H. von Staden

10L

D1564516

HEFFER REISSUES OF STANDARD BOOKS

STOICS AND SCEPTICS

FOUR LECTURES DELIVERED IN OXFORD
DURING HILARY TERM 1913 FOR THE
COMMON UNIVERSITY FUND

BY

EDWYN BEVAN

CAMBRIDGE
W. HEFFER AND SONS, LTD.
1959

ORIGINAL EDITION : 1913 (Clarendon Press)

Photographically reprinted without alteration
for W. Heffer & Sons, Ltd. : 1959

Printed in Great Britain by Lowe and Brydone (Printers) Ltd.
London, N.W.10

PREFACE

THE following four lectures make no pretence of being an exhaustive account of ancient Stoicism and Scepticism. If they attain any measure of success, it is rather as an impressionist sketch than as a photograph. How far the picture is a true one can be judged only by the impression which other people get, looking at the documents as a whole. One hopes, of course, that to some people who come to the fragmentary records of these two schools for the first time, such a sketch may be useful, as giving them a point of view and some general notion of what to look for. Would it be too ambitious to hope that some people familiar already with the ancient philosophies might go back to the documents and find some things stand out in a fresh light?

For those unfamiliar with the field, who may wish to pursue the subject further than four brief lectures can take them, some indication of the books I have found useful may be welcome. The fundamental Zeller goes without saying. The best books—or what appear such to me—upon Stoicism are German: A. Bonhöffer's *Epictet und die Stoa* and *Die Ethik des Stoikers Epictet*. These two are practically two volumes of one work, with an index in common. Bonhöffer has supplemented them by a third smaller book, *Epictet und das Neue*

Testament, which may be recommended to any one interested in the question, What did primitive Christianity owe to its Hellenistic environment?—a vexed question nowadays. The worst book upon Stoicism which I know is also German, L. Stein's *Die Psychologie der Stoa.* Its badness is in part the consequence of the very uncertain hold its author has upon the Greek language. Curiously enough, this book seems to be one to which English writers on Stoicism refer particularly often as an authority, under the impression perhaps that anything written in German has standard worth. Those beginning the study of the subject should be warned. The exposition of Stoicism in these lectures owes a good deal to Heinrich Gomperz's book *Die Lebensauffassung der griechischen Philosophen.* This is a vigorous and interesting defence of a certain attitude to the world. When Gomperz represents that attitude as being precisely the attitude of the ancient Stoics, he is, I think, open to criticism, but, even so, it seems to me that he has helped me to understand the true inwardness of ancient Stoicism better than I should have done otherwise. For Posidonius and the Middle Stoa, A. Schmekel's *Die Philosophie der mittleren Stoa* (1892) is now *the* book. In French there is a readable monograph by F. Ogereau, *Essai sur le système philosophique des Stoïciens* (1885). In English, two books on Stoicism have been produced in recent years, Professor W. L. Davidson's *The Stoic Creed* (1907) and Professor E. Vernon Arnold's *Roman Stoicism* (1911). If the only references to them in the following lectures express dissent, I hope I shall not be understood to deny the merits of either work. The points on which one feels in disagreement are naturally the points where one is moved to speak. When one assents, no remark seems called for. Mr. St. George Stock's little book, *Stoicism*, in Constable's *Philosophies Ancient and Modern*, and Mr. R. D. Hicks's *Stoic and Epicurean* (1910) in the *Epochs of Philosophy* series (Longmans), may also be read with profit. On the subject of Posidonius and the later Hellenistic theology, Professor Gilbert Murray's third lecture in his recently published book, *Four Stages of Greek Religion*, should by no means be overlooked. It will take many people for the first time into a dim world which is only beginning to be explored, and they could have no more delightful *mystagogos* than Professor Murray. A pupil is not in a position to dispense praise to his master, but he may express gratitude. The texts upon which a study of the Old Stoa must be based have been collected by Hans von Arnim (*Stoicorum veterum fragmenta*, Leipzig, vol. i, 1905; vols. ii and iii, 1903). There is an earlier collection of the fragments of Zeno and Cleanthes, by A. C. Pearson (Cambridge University Press, 1891), still useful because of the commentary by which the texts are accompanied. References to earlier writers on Stoicism (Ravaisson, Hirzel, &c.) will be furnished in the works I have mentioned to those who wish to push their studies into the older literature of the subject.

So much for the Stoics. For the Sceptics, Zeller again of course. A recent book dealing specially with the Sceptics is A. Goedeckmeyer's *Geschichte des griechischen Skeptizismus* (Leipzig, 1905). The book is somewhat pedantic in its classifications and wayward in the position which it assigns to Cicero, but apart from that its judgements seem to me sound, and it puts together the material in a form which workers in this part of the field are likely to find signally helpful.

Besides monographs devoted specially to Stoicism or Scepticism there are, of course, numerous works of larger compass dealing with these schools as part of their subject. Zeller has been already referred to. One may also recommend students to consult the histories of philosophy by Döring (1903), Windelband (3rd ed. 1912), and Ueberweg (10th ed. 1909), the relevant part of Hans von Arnim's contribution to Hinneberg's *Kultur der Gegenwart* (Teil i, Abtheilung v, *Allgemeine Geschichte der Philosophie*, 1909), P. Wendland's *Die hellenistisch-römische Kultur* (1907), and Chapter II in Mr. T. R. Glover's *The Conflict of Religions in the Early Roman Empire* (1909).

It remains only for me to express my sense of the honour done me by the Delegates of the Common University Fund, to whose invitation it was due that these lectures were delivered, and my sense of obligation to those friends without whose encouragement they would never have seen the light.

February, 1913.

CONTENTS

LECTURE I

LECTURE I

ZENO AND THE STOA

LECTURE I

ZENO AND THE STOA

THERE is a scene familiar to our imaginations from childhood. We see a wandering Semitic teacher arraigned before the clever, inquisitive people of Athens. Somewhere in the background are the great Periclean buildings which crown the Acropolis. The Semite is declaring to the men of Athens that the Deity dwells not in temples made with hands, is not confined in His dealings to one race, but is the Father of all mankind—an atmosphere, as it were, in which they live and move about and exist, without any such material shape as can be portrayed in metal or stone, the work of human art. About 350 years before Paul of Tarsus passed through Athens, another Semitic teacher, coming from a country close to Cilicia—from Cyprus, and from a city which, like Tarsus, was an old Oriental city penetrated by Hellenism—had gone about among the people of Athens, as clever and inquisitive in that age as in the days of Paul, and had declared to them that the Deity was One Power, pervading the Universe, and dwelling in all men everywhere, without distinction of race, and that in the ideal city there would be no temples, because no temple, the work of builders and artificers, could be worthy of

God.[1] It is a remarkable case of history repeating itself
—the same background and so great similarity between
the actors three and a half centuries apart. Of course
the resemblance between Zeno, the Hellenized Phoenician of Citium, and Paul, the Hellenized Hebrew of
Tarsus, is not purely accidental. The author of the
Acts has assuredly put into the mouth of his Paul, with
deliberate purpose, phrases characteristic of the teaching
which went back to Zeno. Nor is the connexion made
by the writer an arbitrary one; it is the index of
a great fact—the actual connexion in history between
Stoicism and Christianity. Looking back, we can see
more fully than was possible at the moment when the
Acts was written, to what an extent the Stoic teaching
had prepared the ground in the Mediterranean lands for
the Christian, what large elements of the Stoic tradition
were destined to be taken up into Christianity. It
remains, all the same, something of a strange coincidence
that the founder of Stoicism should have come of a race
whose language was almost identical with Hebrew, and
from a Greek-Oriental city so near to Tarsus. The
connexion of Stoicism with that region was always a
close one. Chrysippus, the 'second Founder' of Stoicism,
as he has been called, came from Cilicia, and his
successor, another Zeno, from Tarsus itself. When
Paul lived in Tarsus, as a young man, it was still one
of the chief seats of the Stoic philosophy.

Citium in Cyprus, the native place of Zeno, had a

---

[1] Ἱερά τε οἰκοδομεῖν οὐδὲν δεήσει· ἱερὸν γὰρ οὐδὲν χρὴ νομίζειν οὐδὲ
πολλοῦ ἄξιον καὶ ἅγιον οἰκοδόμων τε ἔργον καὶ βαναύσων. Arnim,
Stoicorum veterum fragm. vol. i, fr. 265.

population which was largely Phoenician in blood. It was ruled by a dynasty of Phoenician petty kings, whose names figure in the Punic inscriptions found on the spot. From 361 to 312 B.C., within which period the first twenty years of Zeno's life probably fall, its king was Pumi-yathon the son of Milk-yathon the son of Baal-ram.[1] That Zeno himself was a Phoenician is implied, I think, in our records. Φοινικίδιον he is called familiarly by his master Krates in one anecdote.[2] Timon the satirist depicts him as an old Phoenician woman.[3] When the charge was brought against him of stealing the doctrines of other schools, his enemies were apt to add 'like a Phoenician'.[4] A group of shrewd Semitic families domiciled in Citium, and doing business round the shores of the Levant—such, we may divine, was the *milieu* whence Zeno came in his youth to fourth-century Athens. It is impossible to harmonize all the stories current in the later tradition about his conversion to philosophy; but one may take as historical, I suppose, the assertion that he first came to Athens on some mercantile enterprise—bringing a cargo of purple from Phoenicia, says one account. At Athens a new world opens for the young man; people here are talking about things larger than commercial gain and loss, and we are shown Zeno going ardently from one philosophic school to another. The atmosphere of Athens at that moment is alive with the philosophic

---

[1] G. A. Cooke, *North Semitic Inscriptions*, p. 55 f.

[2] Diog. Laert. vii. 3.

[3] Timon Phliasius, *Sill.* frag. 20, Wachsmuth.

[4] Diog. Laert. vii. 25.

movement initiated a few generations before by Socrates.
Plato has probably been dead only some thirty years;
and the impression of his personality is still preserved
by men who knew the Master's living presence.
The rivalry between the different schools keeps discus-
sion keen. And Zeno seems to have given them all a
hearing—Crates the Cynic, Stilpo the Megarian, the
successors of Plato in the Academy. At last he came
to feel that he himself had a message to deliver, and we
are shown him walking up and down the Painted Porch,
arguing energetically and somewhat annoyed at the
people who impeded his progress. He is reported on
one occasion to have pointed to the wooden basis of an
altar which was visible at the extremity of the Stoa.
'This once stood in the middle of the Stoa; it was
removed out there, because it got in people's way;
please apply the principle to yourselves.' [1]

Zeno made Athens his second home: he lived there
as a *metoikos* to a good old age; but he felt a bond
of piety still tie him, we are told, to the old city in
Cyprus whence he had come; when his name was put
up in some public inscription at Athens as 'Zeno the
philosopher', they added 'of Citium' at his own request. [2]
He felt that his duty to Citium made it incumbent upon
him to refuse the citizenship which Athens was ready to
bestow. [3] Of the books which he wrote nothing survives
but the titles and a few detached phrases; our knowledge
of his life is confined to a number of miscellaneous
anecdotes, in which the inventiveness of the Athenian

[1] Diog. Laert. vii. 14.   [2] Diog. Laert. vii. 12.
[3] Plut. *De Sto. Rep.* 4.

story-tellers may have had a part impossible now to check.   Yet even an invented story will probably have been *ben trovato*, and through our fragmentary record we may still, I think, get the impression of a real man. The Stoic tradition, which counted for so much in the world of later antiquity, was like other movements of the human spirit in this also : although its development and success can be in large measure accounted for by the conditions of the time, by the receptiveness of the world at that particular moment for that particular thing, still it owed its first impulse not to any conjunction of impersonal causes, but to a human person of singular individuality and force.

It is obvious that Zeno in the later part of his life was one of the considerable figures at Athens, a man to whom the city as a whole turned in political emergencies, to whom kings like Antigonus and Ptolemy paid court.   Something un-Hellenic there must have been in his appearance to the end, an Asiatic darkness of skin, a long, straggling, ungainly body, noticeable among men who had been shaped from youth up by the exercises of the gymnasium.   Among all the Greek teachers it was the Cynics whom he had found most congenial, the men who had set themselves rudely against all that adornment and amenity of life which went with the Hellenic spirit, and had proclaimed every distinction between man and man conventional and worthless.   In a society where pleasure was pursued with artistic elaborations and refinements, there was something bare and gaunt[1]—or

---

[1] Εὐτελὴς τε σφόδρα καὶ βαρβαρικῆς ἐχόμενος μικρολογίας, προσχήματι οἰκονομίας.   Diog. Laert. vii. 16.

was it something impressively plain ?—in the life of the man whose food was so spare that the comedians said he taught his disciples to be hungry, and who seemed to have no use for the services of slaves. 'More self-restrained than Zeno' (Ζήνωνος ἐγκρατέστερος) became a proverbial phrase in Athens.[1] But it was rather the reduction of life to a homely simplicity than any set mortification of the flesh, for Zeno was ready to grow genial over the wine-cups, observing that there was a bitter sort of beans which became pleasant when moistened.[2]

From some of the little characteristics recorded of him we may, I think, realize his individuality. He had learned from the Cynics a bluntness of speech which outraged polite convention. And he delivered himself with a dogmatic conviction, having a peculiar way of throwing his assertions into the form of short compact arguments, of hard syllogisms, which gave them an appearance of mathematical certainty. 'It is reasonable to honour the gods : it would not be reasonable to honour beings which did not exist : therefore the gods exist.'[3] 'Nothing destitute of consciousness and reason can produce out of itself beings endowed with consciousness and reason : the Universe produces beings endowed with consciousness and reason : therefore the Universe is itself not destitute of consciousness and reason.'[4] He

[1] Diog. Laert. vii. 27.

[2] Καὶ οἱ θέρμοι πικροὶ ὄντες βρεχόμενοι γλυκαίνονται. Arnim, *Stoicorum veterum fragm.* vol. i, fr. 285.

[3] Sext. Emp. *adv. math.* ix. 133 = frag. 152, Arnim.

[4] 'Nihil quod animi quodque rationis est expers, id generare ex se

used the Greek language with little regard for Attic sensi-
bilities—whether because he had never quite acquired
the fine instinct of a native or because he scorned grace
of speech—forcing strange new terms to carry the
thoughts which had somehow to be uttered. One
thinks of Carlyle, only this was a Carlyle with con-
centration instead of diffuseness. His huge earnestness
expressed itself in vigorous gesture. We are told how
he used to illustrate the *katalēptikē phantasia*, the impression which gets a grasp on reality, by clenching his
fist.[1]

It is impossible to give such an account of Stoicism
as shall separate clearly the teaching of the founder
from later developments, because any characteristic of the
Stoic tradition was apt to be loosely ascribed to Zeno,
and we cannot now disentangle the original teaching
from the new elements incorporated with it by his successors, especially by the great persevering systematizer,
Chrysippus. The titles of Zeno's works cover a wide
field—metaphysics, logic, physics, ethics, rhetoric—and
this implies a solid body of positive doctrine to which
the later teaching upon a large number of cardinal points
must have remained tied down. But one knows how a
difference of emphasis, of tone, may utterly change any
statement, and one may suspect that Stoicism, seen, as
we must see it, through the somewhat pedantic medium
of Chrysippus, is not quite what it would appear to us,

potest animantem compotemque rationis. Mundus autem generat
animantes compotesque rationis. Animans est igitur mundus composque
rationis.' Cic. *De nat. deor.* ii. 22.

[1] Cic. *Acad. Pr.* ii. 144 = frag. 66, Arnim.

if we could recover the writings of the founder and understand in what context of thought and emotion those phrases were first flung forth, out of which the well-known Stoic paradoxes were framed. We must be content, as it is, to take the Stoic teaching in the form in which it issued from the laboratory of Chrysippus, as a whole, without hoping to distinguish, except very conjecturally, what it was at its first beginning, with Zeno, with Cleanthes.

There is one question about it which naturally suggests itself at the outset, and which has been repeatedly asked: Was the teaching of Zeno a pure development of Hellenic philosophy, or did it owe elements to his Phoenician home ? Those who maintain that the philosophy of Zeno was purely Hellenic can no doubt show how each part of it was connected with the previous philosophic tradition in Greece, and according to the stories, of course, the impulse which turned the young merchant into a philosopher came not from his home influences, but from the Athenian schools. Everybody would nevertheless admit some new and distinctive element in Zeno's teaching, and it may be asked whether this distinctive element had affinities with Eastern lore. Personally, I do not think that the question can ever be answered, for the simple reason that we do not know anything about the wisdom of the Phoenicians. It is idle to discuss whether a child resembles its mother, if there is no means of finding out what the mother was like. Men indeed had thought about life and written books for centuries in the Nearer East: we have Babylonian and Assyrian clay-tablets, we have numerous

sacred writings of the Hebrews ; and this may be enough
to enable the people who operate with the vague and
unserviceable concept of 'Oriental' to theorize confi-
dently about a non-Hellenic element in Stoicism. It
would, however, be most unsafe to deduce the prevalent
conceptions among the Phoenicians in the fourth century
B.C. from the fragments of cuneiform writings ; and the
Hebrews, we know, felt themselves in many ways
the antithesis of the surrounding peoples. That the
Phoenicians had a traditional wisdom of their own is
indeed probable; such 'Wisdom' literature as is exemplified among the Hebrews by the Book of Proverbs
or Job may have had parallels among the Northern
Semites. But it would not be wise to build much
upon such a mere possibility.

But if we are unable to show that the matter of Zeno's
teaching owed anything to a Semitic tradition, we may,
I think, see something in the manner of it which makes
Zeno differ from the established type of Greek philosopher by an approximation to the Eastern prophet.
Or perhaps one should not say *Eastern* prophet, because
the Greek philosopher was a peculiar product of Hellenism within the last two or three centuries, and
the other, the prophetic type of teacher, was found
generally among mankind outside the Hellenic sphere,
even to some extent within it, if we may take Pythagoras,
for instance, or Empedocles as an example. One only
calls the type Eastern because in the Near East it
remained the standard type of teacher, whereas it was
superseded in Hellenism by the philosopher. The pro-
phets are those, to quote Seeley's description in *Ecce*

Homo, 'who have seemed to themselves to discover truth, not so much by a process of reasoning as by an intense gaze, and who have announced their conclusions in the voice of a herald, using the name of God and giving no reasons.' The Greek type of philosopher had reached its completion in Socrates and Plato with their *eirōneia,* their apparent tentativeness of assertion, their placing themselves on a common footing with their hearers. Plato characteristically represented the discovery of truth not as a process in which one proclaimed and the other believed, but as a conversation in which truth, latent in the mind, was elicited by rational argument. This is the very opposite of the prophet's 'Thus saith the Lord'. The prophet and philosopher speak in quite different tones of voice. Now the curious thing about Zeno, it seems to me, is that while his message was Hellenic, his tone of voice was that of the prophet. He had something positive to say, something he wished men to believe, and he conformed to the Hellenic requirements in throwing his message, as we have seen, into the form of brief syllogistic arguments. But one has only to look at those laconic, clenched syllogisms to see that they have by themselves no cogency. They were merely a vehicle for the intense convictions of the teacher. His teaching was essentially dogmatic, authoritative. He named Reason, yes : but in what manner? One might perhaps express the singular combination of manner and matter in his message by saying that its burden was 'Thus saith Reason'. If men received it, it was not because they were convinced in a cold intellectual way, but because behind his affirmations there was a tremendous personal force, because something deep in their own hearts rose up to bear witness to the things he affirmed. It was the way of faith.

We cannot make Zeno himself responsible for the great scholastic system framed by Chrysippus, for all the dogmas and paradoxes which were part of the stereotyped Stoic doctrine later on, but we have every reason to believe that the peculiar features which distinguished Stoicism were due to Zeno, and that the founder's teaching was essentially dogmatic and paradoxical. It seems to me a mistake when, in order to accommodate it to our ways of thinking, its peculiarities are minimized and its characteristics toned down, as if what it meant were really something quite ordinary and common sense. I think it really meant something violent : only its violence may be sympathetically construed, if we understand the urgency which lay upon it. Dogma in our days suggests an unnecessary intellectual garment which trammels and incommodes the mind : we hardly realize the bitter need for dogma felt by minds which have been stripped shivering naked. We must consider at what a moment in the history of ancient civilization Zeno of Citium appeared.

The culture of the Greeks was a development of the last two or three centuries only. Mankind had been many thousands of years on the earth, and for the last few thousand years there had been great civilizations, with arts and literatures and laws. But in these last ten generations, with the Hellenes, a new thing had come to exist, or rather a quality in human nature had been developed to an effectiveness and power never known before—the quality which we describe as Rationalism. The ancestors of the Hellenes, like the rest of mankind, had lived in societies each of which maintained a firm tradition for its members as to the powers operative in the world and as to the binding rules of conduct. To say that every individual had accepted, as a matter of course, the view of the world and the rules of conduct prevalent in his society would be too much ; for there had always, no doubt, been individuals who questioned points in the tradition and opposed or evaded particular rules. But among the Greeks such questioning had come to be systematic and extensive ; it was not the case of an individual revolting, but of a new tradition of free inquiry growing up in the midst of the society, a recognition of Reason as superseding tradition in all departments of life, a clearer distinction between the real facts of the world and the work of human imagination than had ever been made before. It had begun, of course, with a few eager spirits, and the new ferment had been confined at first to little groups of inquirers and disciples, but with the Sophistic movement in the fifth century B.C. it had run everywhere through the Greek world. You know how that made everything seem in flux, everything uncertain. Even the ordinary man in fifth-century Athens became aware that clever people no longer believed in his old gods and his old standards of right and wrong. And in the time of Zeno, scepticism was not only an abstract theory. Those were the days of the Greek conquest of the East, when the individual adventurer was finding larger and larger scope ; there was plenty of the practical scepticism of the man who had

no pretensions to being a philosopher, but only knew
that he could follow his egoistic will without troubling
himself about the gods.   Socrates, indeed, and Plato
had seemed to lay in the midst of this confusion the
foundation for new positive knowledge and morality.
But one must not suppose that the Socratic schools had
put an end to the Sophistic unrest.   To meet a wide popular need, Platonism was too fine-drawn, too abstruse,
too tentative.   Such a general break-up of tradition was
one of the things which this new Rationalism in the Greek
world had brought about.   The situation was one which
no human society, I think we may say, had before in the
world's history been called upon to face.

We must consider that the tradition which in old days
had enclosed each individual from his birth up, fashioning
his ideas of the world, giving him fixed rules for conduct,
had supplied a need.   And the need remained.   It was
not merely that the explanation of the world contained
in the old mythology had been found absurd, and
that man was left confronted with an unsolved enigma.
That might in itself be. unpleasant ; man has a disinterested curiosity ; and an unsolved enigma means
intellectual discomfort.   But man might have put up
with that and acquiesced in agnosticism, if the problem
had been stationary, simply to understand what the
world is here and now.   It was Time which made the
poignancy of the need.   The reality with which men
were confronted was a moving one ; they were being
carried onward, each one into a future of unknown
possibilities, and whatever might lie on the other side of
death, the possibilities on the hither side were disquieting

enough in the fourth century B.C. Even in our firmly
ordered and peaceful society, hideous accidents may
befall the individual; but in those days, when the world
showed only despotic monarchies and warring city-states,
one must remember that slavery and torture were con-
tingencies which no one could be sure that the future
did not contain for him. Now the old tradition had
made man feel that this movement, in which he was
borne along, was subject to the will of beings kindred
to himself. The gods might be envious and vindictive,
but there was a mind and heart there to appeal to,
not altogether unlike the human—there was something
with which man might establish friendly relations and be
at peace. If all that faded into an empty dream, man
found himself left naked to fortune. With the mass
of passionate desires and loves he carried in his heart,
the unknown chances of the future meant ever-present
fear. Unless he could find his good and possess it in such
a way that no conceivable horror which might spring
upon him out of that Unknown could touch it, fear must
be always there, in the background of his thoughts.
This Fear, as we shall see, was one of the constituents of
human misery specially noted in the Stoic school, one
of the things from which Zeno promised deliverance.

But it was something more than relative security in
looking forward into the future which the old tradition
had afforded. Besides giving a certain view of the
world, it had given rules of conduct, standards of
behaviour. And the most imperative reason why man
could not simply discard the old tradition and remain
contentedly agnostic is found here. It was not only

that the reality confronting him was in movement, and that the possibilities of the future for himself made him fearful. This fear, even if a worse agony than mere intellectual discomfort before an unsolved enigma, might have been borne perforce, if man had been simply passive. The important thing was that man was not the passive spectator of a process : he did not only look at Reality ; he helped to make it. He was compelled, whether he wished or not, to act, each fresh minute of his conscious life. And his voluntary action could not be other than purposive : that is to say, in making new Reality, he was obliged to have regard not only to what existed already, but to what ought to exist, to Values, to Good. Every voluntary action implies a value-judgement. The old tradition gave each individual a body of value-judgements in all that the social code called good. And besides stamping certain sorts of behaviour as good in themselves, good in the sense of praiseworthy, the old tradition had coupled extrinsically the goods which were the common objects of human desire—pleasure, health, riches, and so on—with the conduct which it approved, by representing the gods as interested in such conduct and as dispensing rewards. The individual had therefore a fairly complete guide for life. But now that all the traditional canons of conduct had been challenged, and the gods had become a doubtful fable, the question what it was good for a man to do clamoured to be answered. The passionate desires and loves which man carried in his heart created indeed values by which the action of mankind, as Zeno looked at it, was everywhere determined. But the result was not happiness. Mankind seemed to be driven hither and thither in a sea of contrary desires; one impulse overrode and frustrated another; the things which men took for good brought them no satisfaction when they were gained; human life was a chaos, in which blind Desire was the propelling force, and action was spasmodic, furious, vain—a misery of craving for ever disappointed and for ever renewed. This blind Desire was the other great constituent, besides the Fear, in that human misery which the gospel of Zeno claimed to meet. And the two so worked together that a remedy for one would cure the other. For if Zeno was able to put man in possession of a good, secure from all the chances of the morrow, then the desire of man need be directed to nothing beyond it. There was no place for either Desire or Fear any more.

It was such a good which Stoicism bade men see within their reach. Zeno asked in effect what happiness really was, and he found it—this is the essential point— not in a particular sort of sensation or sum of sensations, as men were apt to suppose, but in an attitude of the Will. A man is happy when what he wills exists. It was in terms of Will that Value was to be interpreted; when Zeno said that this or that was a *good*, he meant this or that leaves the Will satisfied. I am happy, when I do not want things to be any other than they are. Among the things present to my consciousness may be a painful sensation; but it is not an evil for me, if it is what I myself will. One may, I think, take as an illustration the painful effort which is felt in athletic exercise; the ache of the muscle is in itself unpleasant, and yet it does not detract from the man's happiness in the moment of his activity; he would not wish it away. Happiness is the correspondence of what exists with the Will, and men whose wills were in bondage to desire tried to find it by shaping outside circumstances according to their desires. This put them at the mercy of fortune and made them slaves to fear. Suppose we brought about the correspondence in another way, by willing what exists? Then, Zeno said, we have a happiness which sets a man free, makes him independent in face of the storms of fortune, extinguishes desire and fear. He feels pain no less than before as an unpleasant sensation, but it is not an evil for him any more, because the attitude of his will towards it is changed. The agony of the rack, of disease, he will feel as the athlete feels his self-chosen effort : he would not have it otherwise. There is the story of Posidonius, the great Stoic of the days of Cicero, receiving a visit from Pompey in Rhodes, whilst suffering from a painful disease. At every fresh spasm which interrupted the conversation, he cried out : 'Do your worst, pain, do your worst : you will never compel me to acknowledge that you are an evil !'[1]—somewhat theatrical, perhaps, but a true declaration of the Stoic principle.

I think one must concede to Zeno that if this adjustment of the Will were carried out, it would do away with fear and entail absolute independence of circumstances. And has one any right to dismiss it straight away as a psychological impossibility? Is it not true that our wills are ours, we know not how? And

---

[1] 'Nihil agis, dolor ! quamvis sis molestus, numquam te esse confitebor malum.' Cic. *Tusc. Dis.* ii. 61.

is it not true that we do sometimes will the painful ? And if we can will the painful in the case of athletic exercise, is it unreasonable to think that we might with determination and practice enlarge our faculty for doing so, even to the point of willing all conceivable pains which might befall us ?   This aspect of the Stoic doctrine has been put forcibly by Heinrich Gomperz in his book *Die Lebensauffassung der griechischen Philosophen*.   Gomperz only regrets that the Stoics coupled their doctrine of redemption by adjustment of the Will with statements about the nature of the Universe.   Their doctrine of redemption, he seems to think, stood strong on its own ground and was only weakened by dogmatic assertions at which the modern agnostic man must naturally shy. I do not know whether this is a view which commends itself to you.   Personally I quite understand that if you are a convinced agnostic, you will have no more use for the Stoic dogma than for any other.   Only I do not see that without such dogma the Stoic precept can be urged with any reason.   Why should I adjust my will to what happens?   Why should I refuse to consider any pain that comes to me an evil?   The Stoic had an answer ready : Because everything that happens is determined by the sovereign Reason.   If you discard the Stoic belief in the Rational Purpose controlling the course of the world, I cannot see why you should call everything that happens to you good.   If the power governing the Universe is represented as an arbitrary Personal Will, one feels that the attitude of Mill, refusing to call good what is not good—'To hell I will go'—is more honourable than a servile acquiescence.   And I do not see that

the attitude of acquiescence becomes any more honourable, if the Universe is driven by blind impersonal forces.
It may be more prudent not to struggle, but it seems a
poor sort of freedom that is won by an acted fiction.

Zeno at any rate felt that his injunction to men to
adjust their wills to the course of the world could only
be reasonably given, if the world were of a certain character. His doctrine, like that of the later Greek philosophical schools in general, was elaborated rather to meet
a practical need than to satisfy speculative curiosity.
But he was just as aware as his contemporary Epicurus
that you cannot have ethical doctrine without a basis of
physical and metaphysical doctrine ; you can have no rule
of conduct without some view of the universe wherein
the action is to take place. He was therefore compelled
to provide an answer to those physical and metaphysical
problems which had been agitating Greek thought.
He had to take the whole field of Greek intellectual
interests into his scope—on Logic, on Rhetoric even, he
had to lay down clear principles. In a system of this
kind, made under such pressure, we must expect to find
that a good deal is put in simply to support the vital
points, to join them up and make the system complete.
And it seems to me that if we are to appreciate the Stoic
system intelligently, we must distinguish the points to
which real importance was attached, the things about
which the constructors really cared, from what one may
call stop-gap theory. One of the reasons, I think, which
often make accounts of Stoicism dull is that a painstaking
student has drawn the Stoic doctrines one by one from
the literary sources and put them together in methodical

order, as if they were all of one quality. Of course, the moment you try to go deeper and understand what were the driving forces in the construction, to distinguish the points about which the teachers cared from the supporting theory, you are on much more conjectural ground. You run the risk of following subjective fancies. But it seems that this risk must be run in all vital interpretations of human work. If you are determined to limit yourself to what is called objective fact, you certainly diminish the chances of your making mistakes, but you also renounce all your chances of getting below the surface. What, for instance, is mainly interesting, to my mind, in the physical theories of Zeno, is not their detail, but the fact that he felt it necessary to enunciate a theory of Nature at all. We cannot understand what he was about unless we realize the necessity which was on him to give a complete answer to the enigma of the Universe, compact in all its parts, since nothing which left any room for doubt to get in could give a bewildered world security and guidance.[1]

Stoicism, as it appears to me, was a system put together hastily, violently, to meet a desperate emergency. Some ring-wall must be built against chaos. High over the place where Zeno talked could be descried

[1] (Cato *loquitur*) 'Verum admirabilis compositio disciplinae incredibilisque me rerum traxit ordo; quem, per deos immortales, nonne miraris? quid enim aut in natura, qua nihil est aptius, nihil discriptius, aut in operibus manu factis tam compositum tamque compactum et coagmentatum inveniri potest? quid posterius priori non convenit? quid sequitur, quod non respondeat superiori? quid non sic aliud ex alio nectitur, ut, si ullam litteram moveris, labent omnia? nec tamen quicquam est, quod moveri possit.' Cic. *De Fin.* iii. 74.

the wall, built generations before, under the terror of a Persian attack, built in haste of the materials which lay to hand, the drums of columns fitted together, just as they were, with the more regular stones. That heroic wall still looks over the roofs of modern Athens. To Zeno it might have been a parable of his own teaching.

Even the passion of the Stoics for definition may in this way be regarded with human sympathy. It began with Zeno himself, who established numerous brief formulae as fixed and canonical definitions in the school tradition. Short definitions of this kind were well adapted to become current coin of all the philosophic schools and even of the market-place. As a matter of fact the Stoic definitions had a wide circulation in later antiquity. It is always the catch-words of a philosophical theory which lay hold of the general mind. Stoicism issued its own catch-words, one might say, with the official stamp. One of Zeno's disciples, Sphaerus, seems to have shown a special aptitude for their manufacture. One is at first inclined to treat all this as a kind of dry philosophical pedantry. Perhaps with Chrysippus and the later Stoics such a vice of the mind was not altogether absent. But I think the motive behind it does take on another, and even a pathetic, aspect, when we consider the necessity to have a cut-and-dried answer ready to every question, if a coherent dogmatic system was to be fitted out such as the ordinary man could grasp, and consider also the bitter need for such a system which the world felt at that time.

We have seen then two of the parts of which Zeno's teaching must necessarily consist—the part which gave direction for conduct, the Ethical part, and the part which gave a theory of the Universe, described in the technical language of the schools as the Physical part. Physics, you will notice, in this extended sense includes Theology. But there was yet a third part—or rather a first and preliminary part—indispensable to the whole. There was the initial difficulty which confronted any and every dogmatic philosophy, the scepticism which had become general in the Greek schools with the activity of speculation and the Sophistic movement. Men were apt to doubt, not only a particular statement as to the nature of the Universe, but whether data existed for making any statement at all. It was especially sense-perception of all kinds which rational criticism had shown fallacious: the delusions of sight and hearing had been urged in such a way that the ordinary man was coming to despair of all knowledge; 'all we have power to see is a straight staff bent in a pool.' Even Plato had agreed with the Sophists in throwing over sense-perception as almost worthless; it is true that he had held out in its place the hope of attaining knowledge by pure Reason, but he had not, as we saw, put forth any body of positive doctrine likely to be popular. The Platonic Ideas the ordinary man would find something insubstantial. All this compelled one who came forward, like Zeno, as a dogmatic teacher, to comprise in his philosophy a theory of knowledge; he must be able to give a clear account of the processes of mind by which we acquire knowledge and utter it when it is acquired. This constituted the first part in Zeno's philosophy, the Logical part as it was called.

Each of the three parts of the Stoic doctrine, the Logical, the Physical, and the Ethical, had its special stumbling-block, a point upon which the hostile critics of antiquity directed their attack. In the Logical part the stumbling-block was the Stoic doctrine of certainty. We could not talk about certainty at all, Zeno may have reasoned, unless we knew in reference to something what certainty meant. There must be something I am sure of to give me my standard. He felt prepared to go even farther, to assert that even in the discredited field of sense-perception we had some certain knowledge. It was all very well for the Sophists to talk about the deceptiveness of the senses, and, of course, we were deceived sometimes; but Zeno, as a plain, honest man, felt it absurd to use these occasional delusions to invalidate sense-perceptions wholesale. In each of these particular cases, if we looked close, we should find some special circumstance which made the perception an abnormal one, such as the watery medium making the straight staff look bent; it is not fair to take it as an instance of normal seeing. We have impressions, as a matter of fact, of whose truth we are quite sure. There are things which come home to us with such distinctness (ἐνάργεια) that to doubt is a physical impossibility. The impression, in a phrase which assuredly goes back to Zeno himself, 'takes hold of us by the hair and drags us to assent.'[1]   The soul,

[1] Μόνον οὐχὶ τῶν τριχῶν, φασί, λαμβάνεται, κατασπῶσα ἡμᾶς εἰς συγκατάθεσιν.   Sext. Emp. adv. math. vii. 257.

Zeno taught, receives impressions (φαντασίαι) as wax receives the impress of the seal. It is hardly credible that the metaphor was received quite literally in the Stoic school, even before Chrysippus definitely explained it as figurative. The impressions, Zeno continued, differ from each other in clearness and sharpness of outline. Some are not clear enough to afford certainty as to the objects whence they come. There is another sort characterized by grasping, comprehension (κατά-ληψις). We come here to the *kataleptikē phantasia*, which held so prominent a place in Stoic doctrine, the impression which leaves no room for doubt. Out of such *phantasiai* all real knowledge is built up. A *kataleptikē phantasia*, we may note at this point, need not necessarily be a sense-impression; it may also be the apprehension of a truth logically deduced from indubitable premisses. In either case, such a *phantasia* is true to objective fact and possessed of convincing force. The ideal Wise Man is characterized on the intellectual side by the sureness with which he distinguishes 'grasping impressions' from ambiguous ones. He is not omniscient, but he is incapable of making a mistake.

Zeno's theory of knowledge is, of course, a naïve one. Certain truths were, I think, working in it. It is true surely that there must be some things we know in order to make it possible for the problem of knowledge to be raised at all. And we must, I suppose, allow that all our knowledge of matters of fact must take its start from concrete experiences which include an element of bodily sensation. And if we call the

straight staff bent in a pool, to take the favourite
Sophistic instance we have already referred to, a fallacious appearance, this means that we contrast it with
other appearances of the staff to sight and touch, which
are more stable and coherent.   It is only because part
of our sense-experience seems relatively trustworthy,
that we discover the deceitfulness of other parts.   And
among the qualities by which in actual life we distinguish
true sense-experience from fallacious, a clearness and
definiteness of character, the Stoic *enargeia*, is unquestion-
ably one.   We may also grant to Zeno that a perfectly
judicious man would never make a mistake.   For the
Stoic did not apparently mean that he would never
adopt an erroneous working hypothesis: only when he
did so, he would be fully aware of its hypothetical
character, and would therefore make no mental assertion
which would be stultified by the event.   A crucial case
was the trick played by King Ptolemy upon Zeno's
disciple Sphaerus, in presenting him at a banquet with
a pomegranate of wax.   When the philosopher tried to
eat it, Ptolemy asked him mockingly whether he had
not assented to a false impression.   No, Sphaerus
answered, he had merely assented to the probability
that the fruit offered him by King Ptolemy was a real
one.[1]   The Wise Man's *assent* (συγκατάθεσις) would
never be given to anything but a *kataleptikē phantasia*.
Only in order that an impression might be *kataleptikē* it
must be clear and complete enough to exclude all
interpretations but one; only one theory as to its origin

---

[1] Diog. Laert. vii. 177.

must be logically possible.[1]   Now we must admit that if there were any mind judicious to the degree of perfection, it would recognize exactly how much the data before it proved, and if there were any impressions of which only one theory was possible, it would embrace that theory with absolute certainty.   Wherever—this is Zeno's point—any one makes a mistake, gives away his full belief to something untrue, we can always find that his judiciousness, and not the data, has been at fault; the data did not compel him to his belief; they left an alternative open of which he omitted to take account. The Stoic school allowed that in the case of a large number of impressions alternatives *were* left open; wisdom then consisted simply in recognizing them, in withholding assent; the Wise Man would in practice follow the probable, knowing it to be probable only. In reference therefore to these the doctrine of the Stoics did not differ from that of the sceptical Academy; both enjoined the same suspense of judgement (ἐποχή). Only the Academy taught that no impressions existed which did not leave alternatives open.   The Stoics maintained that some impressions there were which could be grasped, upon which the Wise Man could rest the weight of his full belief and upon which he could build a system of certain knowledge.

The general proposition that human experience furnishes some data upon which we can rely as true must be admitted by every one who does not deny the existence of knowledge altogether.   When we go on

---

[1] Ἡ ἀπὸ ὑπάρχοντος ὁποία οὐκ ἂν γένοιτο ἀπὸ μὴ ὑπάρχοντος, Arnim, *Stoicorum veterum fragm.* vol. i, fr. 59.

to ask what these data are, the real difficulties begin. This is where the *naïveté*, the crudity of the Stoic epistemology becomes apparent. Zeno seems to have distinguished ' grasping impressions' from ambiguous ones only in the most rough-and-ready fashion. He confounded the feeling of assurance, the psychological fact, with logical justification. To say that there were impressions which we could not help believing was really no answer to the critical question, What ought we to believe ? Zeno probably never understood the real meaning of the sceptical inquiry. His motive was not speculative but practical. Dialectic had value for him simply as a means for beating down the objections raised against any dogmatic system at the threshold. If an opponent could show that no perceptions yielded certain knowledge, the claims of the dogmatic teacher collapsed at once. To establish therefore the bare general truth that some indubitable perceptions, some *kataleptikai phantasiai*, existed was itself to clear the ground. We can understand perhaps the impatience with which Zeno brushed aside the cobwebs of the Sceptics, as an offence to the healthy human understanding, by looking at the line taken by Epictetus in the matter.[1] Epictetus assuredly only reproduced in this

---

[1] Ἔτι τούτῳ διαλέγομαι; καὶ ποῖον αὐτῷ πῦρ ἢ ποῖον σίδηρον προσαγάγω, ἵν' αἴσθηται ὅτι νενέκρωται; αἰσθανόμενος οὐ προσποιεῖται· ἔτι χείρων ἐστὶ τοῦ νεκροῦ, i. 5, 7. Ἐρχέσθω καὶ ἀπαντάτω Πυρρώνειος καὶ Ἀκαδημαϊκός. ἐγὼ μὲν γὰρ τὸ ἐμὸν μέρος οὐκ ἄγω σχολὴν πρὸς ταῦτα κτλ., i. 27, 15. Οὐ μᾶλλον ἢ οἱ ἀταλαίπωροι Ἀκαδημαϊκοὶ τὰς αἰσθήσεις τὰς αὑτῶν ἀποβαλεῖν ἢ ἀποτυφλῶσαι δύνανται, καίτοι τοῦτο μάλιστα πάντων ἐσπουδακότες, ii. 20, 20. These are typical expressions of an antipathy which is always breaking out in Epictetus.

point the temper which the Stoic school had inherited
from its founder. Zeno overbore the sceptical arguments
by the drive of his positive conviction. The purport
of all his logical theory was to give men courage to
embrace with full assurance the Truth which he had come
to proclaim concerning Nature and God and Man.

What then was the Truth according to Zeno? We
discover in the department of Physics no less than in
that of Logic a practical rather than a speculative interest
as the determining motive in Stoicism. It was not that
Zeno addressed himself to the Universe with a pure
disinterested curiosity to know the truth of things for
the sake of knowing, but he wanted to make sure of
such things about it as should justify a certain emotional
and volitional attitude in men. The whole of the Stoic
Physics was directed to showing that the Power operative in the Universe was rational: all its theory of the
constitution of the material world and the course of
its movement led up to that crowning result. The
actual detail of the Stoic cosmogony, so far as we can
recover it, does not contain anything very original or
interesting. Zeno seems to have done little more than
take over the tradition of the old Ionian philosophers.
Their conception of Nature had been, as is well known,
the one described as Hylozoïsm. They thought, that
is, of the Reality underlying the changing manifold of
the sensible world as a *Physis*, a material stuff, which had
the characteristics of life. Heraclitus seems to have
identified this stuff, described, of course, as fire, with
Logos, Reason, the orderly Law which governed the
process of unending change. To us the metaphysical

grossness of identifying Consciousness, or any element in Consciousness, with a material substance is so obvious that it is difficult for us to transport ourselves into a phase of thought when such confusion was possible. And when Zeno came to Athens, there had already been Plato to lay stress upon the incorporeal character of the Soul and of the world of Ideas. But the Phoenician did not find satisfaction in concepts so impalpable ; he harked back to the older Ionian doctrine. For him too the whole Universe was only one Substance, one *Physis*, in various states, and that one substance was Reason, was God. He seems to have stated that God and the Soul were *bodies*, as emphatically as the Platonists stated that they were *unbodily*. This was the great stumbling-block of Stoicism in the department of Physics. Zeno was determined all through, as has been said, by a practical motive, and when he said ' God is Body ', what we may discern is, I think, his repugnance to any teaching which would dissolve God into an abstract idea ; it was the crude expression of an intense conviction that God was real, was concrete. We must remember too that Platonism had banished God from the material world, had left it a dark mass from which the Soul must detach itself if it would find Him, and yet this is the world which encloses us on every side, with which we have primarily to do. Zeno came, as it were, to men asking where they could find God and struck his hand upon the solid earth and answered ' Here '. There was nothing which was not, in its ultimate origin, God ; it was He in whom man lived and moved and had his being.

Zeno taught that God is Body, but it was not a dead stuff which constituted the world. The thing which Zeno was concerned above all others to affirm was that this stuff was actually Reason. The Universe is a living being (ζῷον); that was the fundamental formula of Stoic Physics. Nothing could be farther from what is understood by Materialism in modern times. The essential point of that is to deny rational purpose in the primary laws governing the world : one state of matter passes into another according to uniformities which leave no room for purpose, which could be stated as a rigid mathematical equation, if we only knew enough. Zeno's essential point, on the other hand, is the identification of the material *Physis* with Reason. This identification is certainly a clumsiness of thought, but it is misleading to speak of the gross Materialism of Stoicism in the same sense in which we call modern Materialism gross. For what really signifies is whether the Universe is or is not directed by rational purpose. The Materialism of Zeno was refined from the moral and practical point of view by the very metaphysical grossness which endued matter with the characteristics of spirit.

The difficulty which immediately confronts all Pantheism is, of course, the choice between making all the Universe *equally* God and so emptying the idea of God of all meaning, and on the other hand recognizing distinctions of more or less divine, which is hard to do if we have begun by declaring that everything which exists is indistinguishably God. Zeno chose the latter alternative. When he spoke of God or Reason as governing the world, he implied the existence of something other than God, something which is governed, passive to God's active. There it was, all this inert matter, which we see and handle and lift and push. And he explained that God in His proper being, in the state which realized all His potentiality, was not the whole of matter but the finest part of it. He described this part, following Heraclitus, as a fire, or as a fiery ether, more subtle than the common air and fire we know. This fiery ether was identical with pure Reason. Somehow part of the fire had got condensed and heavy and lost its divinity. Zeno gave an account, modelled on the old Ionian physics, of how this world came about, how part of the divine fire became depotentiated and changed into the grosser elements, the common fire which burns, air, water, and earth. Part, however, of the original fiery ether retained its proper form, and this constituted the active power in the Universe, whilst the rest was the passive material upon which it acted. All round the world was an envelope of the fiery ether, pure and unmixed, but it also penetrated the whole mass, as its soul. The orderly working of Nature was its operation : organic beings grew according to regular types, because the Divine Reason was in them as a *logos spermatikos*, a *formula* of life developing from a germ. Even upon earth some of the divine fire retained its pure essence—the reasonable souls, each one a particle of fiery ether, which dwelt in the hearts of men.[1]

---

[1] I say nothing here about the doctrine of τόνος, because I do not understand it. It is not clear to me that τόνος in this connexion meant 'tension', or that it was so prominent a part of the Stoic physics as modern books make out.

It was to a Universe so conceived that Stoicism bade men surrender their wills. Every movement in the world was as much the expression of a Supreme Purpose as the voluntary movements of an animal were of its individual purpose. Chance had no place in the close-knit process which might be called Fate or Destiny (εἱμαρμένη), but which was really Intelligent Law and all-pervading Providence (πρόνοια). It was for the faith in Providence above all else that the Stoic stood in the ancient world.

LECTURE II

THE STOA (*continued*)

LECTURE II

THE STOA (*continued*)

WE saw in our previous lecture how the decay of the old traditional beliefs, of the old traditional rules of conduct, had left a great part of Greek society at the beginning of the third century B.C. without a fixed guide for life. The question 'What is good for the sons of men which they should do under the heaven all the days of their life?' was a question which faced many individuals in those days of adventure and movement, and a question which many answered by blind impulse and at haphazard. It was at such a moment that a teaching began to go out into the world with the promise of tranquillity and guidance, the teaching first expounded by Zeno of Citium in the Painted Porch at Athens. We saw in our previous lecture how Zeno had shown men a way of escape from Fear and Desire by the adjustment of their wills to everything which the course of the world brought upon them, and how he could bid them to adjust their wills because the course of the world was in every detail governed by the same Divine Reason that dwelt in their own breasts.

Reason? Yes, but what did this mean? This surely is just one of the points where Stoicism, in its haste to construct a dogmatic system for popular use, stops short with a vague and unanalysed concept. Reason was a term taken up from current phraseology, a term which people felt they understood, and which gave them a happy sense of security, but which meant much or little according to the context.   It meant sometimes the logical consistency of judgements, the coherence of a train of argument, but as applied to action that meaning could not suffice.   When we ask the *reason* of an action, we inquire about its end or purpose, and we call the action reasonable in two senses—(1) if its end or purpose is a worthy one, and (2) if it is itself adapted to secure the end it aims at.   If the assertion 'The Universe is directed by Reason' were intended in the latter sense only, it would mean just this : 'The Universe is governed by a Purpose of some kind and all events that happen are means adapted to secure its realization.' This assertion by itself would give no ground for the glad acceptance enjoined by Stoicism.   It would not imply that the Purpose was a good one ; it would not even exclude the possibility that the world was governed by a malignant Power.   The Stoic must therefore have meant by his assertion, not only that the events of the world were directed by a Providence to realize a certain Purpose, but that the Purpose was a worthy one.   He attributed, that is to say, value to the End towards which the Universe moved.   Reason means in this case the apprehension of values.   But value is something which has relation to persons.   It would be no reason for my assenting joyfully to the Universe, if the value it secured were not what I understood by value.   The Stoic teaching would accord with this statement, for it was one of the things most insisted upon in Stoicism that the reason in the individual breast was homogeneous with, of one substance with, the Supreme Reason in the Universe.   It implied that the values which I, as a reasonable being, recognize are those to which the whole reasonable Universe is directed.   That is why I can joyfully assent to whatever happens.   It is the working out of a good which I recognize in myself as good.   But what is the nature of this good ?   It is no use to look for answers to this question in the Stoic writings.   Stoicism will go no farther than the bare assertion : The Universe is directed to realize a value which you, as a human being, could appreciate, if you knew the whole.   That is all that its statement, 'The Universe is reasonable,' can be made to yield.

One can understand the void which was thus left in the Stoic teaching by comparing it at this point with Christianity.   Here, too, we find the faith that the Universe is governed by a Purpose towards a valuable end, but Christianity gives a positive image of this end by describing it as Love.   In the relation of love between spiritual beings in this world, broken and imperfect as it is, the Christian holds that we see something whose completion and perfection is ' that divine far-off event to which the whole creation moves '.   There is nothing in this inconsistent with the Stoic faith, The Universe is reasonable ; only the Stoic presents, as it were, an empty form which the Christian fills with positive content. I don't wish to raise the question now whether the Christian is justified in doing so, or whether it is wiser to stop where the Stoic does, with a mere formal assertion.   I want only to show that the Stoic does stop short.

He tells us that the world-process realizes value of some kind, value which we could appreciate, and he tells us no more.

He tells us, I mean, nothing about the inner meaning of the world-process; about the process, looked at from outside as a series of events in time, the Stoic was more ready to make dogmatic affirmations than the Christian. Zeno taught that the present state of things, in which part of the Divine had sunk to the condition of inert matter and part had been distributed as individual souls, would cease by all being reabsorbed once more into the fiery Ether, which is Reason and God. God would again be all in all, a uniformity which excluded all inner diverseness, a homogeneous mass of pure fire. On its material side the doctrine conveys an apprehensible meaning; we can picture more or less a huge fiery sphere in empty space. On its spiritual side, it is harder to make sense of. For, to begin with, we can do little with a conception which identifies Reason with a material substance. And to speak of pure Reason existing by itself in an undifferentiated unity is to use words which convey nothing, I think, to the mind. Reason, we have seen, means primarily in this case the apprehension of values, and the Stoic gives us no hint what values the Divine Mind in its solitary oneness could apprehend.

Zeno did not, however, hold that the absorption of the Universe in the Primal Fire would be for ever. It is not easy for the speculative mind to rest in any limit as ultimate, and the thinker who had followed the world-process to its conflagration in God was left still straining his thought beyond. There was one way of obviating the discomfort of an absolute end. And this was to make the movement of the world circular. What had happened once could happen again. And beyond the period of unification in the Divine Fire Zeno forecast the beginning of another world-process which would follow exactly the same course as the present one and end, like it, in the one Fire. And so on for ever—for the present process was one of an infinite recurrent series — an everlasting, unvarying round. We may wonder that the human mind has acquiesced in such a view of things, even when we allow for its recoil from the notion of an absolute end; but it has done so, not in Greece only, but in India, and even in modern Europe. Those, however, in modern Europe who have embraced the hypothesis of the Eternal Recurrence have never pretended to regard the world-process as governed by rational purpose. In Stoicism the view is eminently incongruous. We are given a Purpose that leads nowhere. This must have made it all the harder to find any meaning in the term Reason, when men were told to assent joyfully to the world-process, with all its pains, because it was Reason which governed the whole.

But all this Stoic doctrine of salvation by acquiescence only met half the need of man. For the experience of each man, the Stoics insisted, was traversed by one broad distinction, the distinction between those parts which the man can control by his will and those parts which are independent of his will. This is the initial distinction with which the ethical doctrine of Stoicism

sets out. A great part of each man's experience
happens to him through no choice of his, through the
play of natural forces, winds and fires and tides, through
the play of thousands of human wills other than his.
Part of his experience, on the other hand, he is conti-
nuously making by his own will.   Strictly speaking, it is
only his own inner dispositions, the Stoics taught, over
which a man has full control. The only thing the
Will can move with absolute security is itself. But it
was nevertheless obvious that to some extent corre-
spondent changes in the external world followed each
man's acts of will, and that we were each of us bound
to will on the supposition that such changes would take
place in consequence of our volition. In so far man
intervened actively in the course of things, and the
precept which bade him adjust his will to accept what
was given could not furnish him with a guide for action.
The Stoic teacher, in cutting off the Fear and Desire
which held men in bondage to the external world, was
suppressing the motives which largely determined the
action of the ordinary man in that field, and he was
bound to find for him some other principle of direction.
True, the traditional code of society stamped certain
sorts of conduct as good and bad respectively, but
this was just one of the things whose authority had
been shaken by the Sophistic inquiry.[1] Man there-

[1] Professor Gilbert Murray has pointed out to me the necessity of
making it clear that the Stoics did not want simply to re-establish the
traditional code of morals. They wanted to find a new basis for
conduct in absolute ' reason '. Their criticism of current moral valua-
tion was in some points, as Professor Murray observes, violently
radical. See *Stoicorum veterum fragm.*, Arnim, vol. i, fr. 249–57.

fore wanted, not only something to give him peace of mind as passive to the overwhelming power of Nature, but something to guide him as active in the natural world.

There is obviously some difficulty in fitting any scheme of action to the Stoic doctrine of salvation by acquiescence. For if I am not to be troubled by the actions of other men because everything that happens is determined by the sovereign Reason to promote its Divine Plan, then it is hard to see why I need take thought for my own action.

Here is a difficulty which Stoicism never satisfactorily explained. It would, however, be hardly fair to reckon this very much to its discredit, since the difficulty in question is really an aspect of the standing problem of Evil, which no religious philosophy has been able to leave anything but a problem still. We may more justly tax Stoicism with not having faced the problem, with having rather glossed it over, or perhaps with never having been aware of it in its real poignancy. The problem of Evil is at its sharpest where the wills of finite individuals come into play. For everything which results from their volition seems on the religious hypothesis to have a double determination, to be determined by the Supreme Will in the Universe, and to be also determined by the finite individual will. If, as determined by the Supreme Will, it is good, how can it ever, as determined by the finite will, be evil? Cleanthes, the first to sit in the chair of the Founder in the Stoic school, skirts the problem in his great hymn :

There is no work done upon earth apart from Thee,
　　O God,
Neither in the divine ethereal sky nor in the sea,
Except what wicked men do in their own folly.

This seems plainly enough to maintain the really evil
character of some human action at the expense of giving
up its determination by God altogether. Cleanthes,
however, tries to save the universality of Divine Providence in the following lines :

But Thou knowest how to make odd things even,
And to order what is disorderly, and unlovely things
　　are lovely to Thee.
For in such wise hast Thou fitted all things together
　　in one, good with evil,
That there results one reasonable design (*logos*) of the
　　whole, enduring for ever.[1]

We see by the end of the hymn that the attitude of Cleanthes in practice and in emotion towards human action
is determined by the view that much, or even most,
of it is really evil. He closes with the urgent prayer to
God for the conversion and salvation of men.[2] We may

---

[1] Οὐδέ τι γίγνεται ἔργον ἐπὶ χθονὶ σοῦ δίχα, δαῖμον,
οὔτε κατ' αἰθέριον θεῖον πόλον οὔτ' ἔνι πόντῳ,
πλὴν ὁπόσα ῥέζουσι κακοὶ σφετέραισιν ἀνοίαις·
ἀλλὰ σὺ καὶ τὰ περισσὰ ἐπίστασαι ἄρτια θεῖναι,
καὶ κοσμεῖν τἄκοσμα καὶ οὐ φίλα σοὶ φίλα ἐστίν·
ὧδε γὰρ εἰς ἓν πάντα συνήρμοκας, ἐσθλὰ κακοῖσιν,
ὥσθ' ἕνα γίγνεσθαι πάντων λόγον αἰὲν ἐόντα.
　　Arnim, *Stoicorum veterum fragm.* vol. i, fr. 537, ll. 11-17.

[2] Ἀλλὰ Ζεῦ πάνδωρε, κελαινεφές, ἀργικέραυνε,
ἀνθρώπους μὲν ῥύου ἀπειροσύνης ἀπὸ λυγρῆς,
ἣν σύ, πάτερ, σκέδασον ψυχῆς ἄπο, δὸς δὲ κυρῆσαι
γνώμης.　　ib., ll. 28-31.

regard this as an outbreak of the human soul, *naturaliter Christiana*, in spite of all intellectual theory. But it certainly seems to imperil the base of the Stoic teaching. For the moment I admit that things over which I have no control, such as other people's action, may be evil, I seem to be back again in the region of Fear and Desire. If on the other hand I hold to the view that no human action is evil, upon what can ethics of any kind be built?

Stoicism had then apparently to desert its base, when it set out to frame a rule for conduct in the world. It had to mark out a right and wrong, and it had to give a motive for action. Why should I engage in action of a particular sort ? The Stoic answer seems to have been somewhat as follows : 'It is true that whatever you do, your action will be found to have subserved the Divine Plan, and so be good from the point of view of a spectator of the whole, but it will make all the difference to you personally whether you fall in willingly with the Divine Reason or struggle against it. It is only when your will is directed in harmony with the Divine Will that you can have peace of mind. And for you such peace is the supreme good, or rather the only good, and disharmony the only evil. But if your will is directed in harmony with God's, a certain sort of conduct will result.'

'In harmony with God's,' we have said, but the Stoic technical phrase was 'in agreement with Nature'. The two phrases for a Stoic would mean the same thing, for by Nature he understood that ruling principle in the Universe which was Reason and God. Only to call it Nature, φύσις, in this connexion indicated usefully its relation to individual things. For the word had come to contain implications such as 'Nature' still has for us. The nature of an individual thing is the normal law of its being; the words 'natural' and 'unnatural' imply that any violation of that law in the case of a conscious being leads to its being in a condition which is somehow wrong and uncomfortable. To the Stoic this multitude of norms applicable to individual things were so many different manifestations of the One Living Reason or Law which governed the Universe. A thing in harmony with its own nature was therefore in harmony with God.

But when was a thing in harmony with its nature? The Stoics answered, 'When it is determined by its own Ruling Principle (ἡγεμονικόν), by the highest thing in it; a plant, for instance, by the principle of vegetable life (which is called "nature" in the narrower sense), a beast by its animal soul, and a man by reason. The "ruling principle" in man is reason, a detached part (ἀπόσπασμα) of the Cosmic Reason. It is therefore well with a man only when his Ruling Principle is in a right state and really governs his being; when that is the case, he possesses all good.'

The right state of a man's Ruling Principle implied action of a particular kind as issuing from it. So far the Stoics were prepared to go in bringing the Wise Man out of an attitude of passive acceptance into action. But they were careful to insist that the state of his Ruling Principle was the Wise Man's only concern. That could be left to him, it seemed, without dragging him back into Fear and Desire, because that was a region wholly in his own power.   He was absolute lord of his own will, but of nothing outside.   And his Ruling Principle was in a right state when it retained its proper condition of pure Reason.

We are once more brought against the concept of Reason as a form which requires content.   For it means, as we saw, the apprehension of true values. When the Stoic said, 'A man should be governed by reason and not passion,' we can only understand it to mean that a man should not allow his perception of true values to be obscured by transient emotions or bodily appetites.   This does not yet tell us what are true values and how they are to be determined.

The Stoics, however, did not leave the concept of Reason as blank in the case of men as they did in the case of God.   They made an attempt to indicate the values which Reason recognized.   And first, a value inhered in the temper itself which the Wise Man maintained, in his fearlessness, his grand independence of the outside world.   These things were good in themselves, with a goodness which could not be demonstrated by logical argument, but only immediately perceived.   The Stoic school, at any rate from the time of Chrysippus, stood for an intuitional element in Ethics.   They gave currency to the phrase 'innate notions' (ἔμφυτοι ἔννοιαι) or preconceptions (προλήψεις).   They did not mean that men brought with them into the world the knowledge of any concrete thing, but that they brought a certain faculty of perceiving values, so as to know goodness when they saw it.   Real good, we have seen, had to be confined to that part of the inner life which was controlled by the Will ; there it could be always within reach. Difficulty arose from the fact that action lay in the outside sphere, and to admit the possibility of a right and a wrong in that action seemed to involve the recognition of a difference of values, a good and a bad, in outside things. This was a great crux for Stoicism, for on no account must the absolute tranquillity and the independence of the Wise Man be disturbed, and yet he must act as if differences between outside things mattered. Stoicism here becomes ingenious.

There is, it says, a difference of value even among things outside the domain of the will ; in fact, the Greek word most corresponding in meaning to our 'value', ἀξία, was introduced by Stoicism into the technical phraseology of the schools with special reference to a quality belonging to outside things, the term ἀπαξία, *unworth*, being coined as its antithesis. Only difference in value in this peculiar sense was not a difference of *good* and *evil*. Nothing was good but the good will, and nothing evil but the bad. 'Mere verbal quibbling,' opponents of Stoicism, like Plutarch, allege. But not justly ; for the attitude of the Wise Man to the inner good—the good which consisted in a certain direction of the will—really was other than his attitude to any outside thing. His attitude towards every outside thing was emptied of desire—that is why they were all alike *indifferent* (ἀδιάφορα) in respect of *good*. His action was not directed upon any outside thing in such a way that he failed, or was disappointed, if his intention was not realized. The point of the Stoics was that a thing may serve

to give direction to action without being an object of
desire.   This is obviously true.   Supposing you are
a servant sent to fetch a parcel from the post office for
your employer, you may be perfectly indifferent as to
whether the parcel has arrived or not ; your whole
action in going to the post office, all the consecutive
movements of your feet, will be directed by an
intention to get the parcel, but if you found that it was
not there, you would feel no disappointment, and rest
satisfied with having fulfilled your part in the business.
That is a type of the attitude of the Stoic Wise Man towards outside things.   There are certain things which
will give direction to his intention.   The things to whose
possession the Wise Man would direct his intention,
but not his desire, Zeno described by the new term of
προηγμένα, things 'promoted' or 'preferred'.   They are
the things which possess ἀξία, 'value,' in the sense we
specified just now.   For the opposite things, those to
avoid which the Wise Man would direct his intention,
but not his desire, which possessed ἀπαξία, unworth, he
coined the ugly term ἀποπροηγμένα, 'dispromoted'.
Health and wealth, for instance, were among the promoted things ; that is to say, they would be to the Wise
Man exactly like the parcel at the post office in our
illustration.   His action would be directed by the
intention of acquiring or keeping them, but no desire
would go with it, so that if he lost health and wealth, it
would be a matter of complete indifference to him ; his
good lay wholly in the right direction of the will, and
that he had secured.   You see that this scheme allows
the Wise Man to engage in selective action without

prejudice to his unchangeable inner tranquillity and freedom.

But on what principle would he select and reject ? If Stoicism was going to furnish a practical guide for action, it must give some clear indication here. It resorted again to the concept of Nature. For a reasonable being only one thing in the strict sense was κατὰ φύσιν, natural, and that was to have its reason in perfect activity. But there was a sense in which certain other conditions or circumstances were 'natural' for it. According to the scheme of things framed by the Universal Reason, constituting Nature, those conditions or circumstances were such that actions directed to secure them were *appropriate* to it (καθήκοντα). There were first the instincts by which human beings in the earliest phase of life, when reason was still undeveloped and they were on the merely animal level, were directed to certain objects (τὰ πρῶτα κατὰ φύσιν). The Stoics specified the great object which the animal, and man in the animal stage, instinctively desired as the conservation of the individual being whole and sound. They were especially opposed to the Epicurean psychology which put Pleasure among these things instinctively sought. Pleasure, they maintained, supervened upon the satisfaction of the instinct, but was not its object. In turning to these objects the living creature was following a law established by Nature as the intelligent orderer of the Universe; when Reason supervened upon animal life, the old law of instinct was superseded by the higher law of Reason, and what had been natural for the animal was no longer natural, in the true sense, for the man. Man would still, however, have a respect for these connexions made by the order of the world, and his will would be in a right attitude, in harmony with Nature, when it was directed by the intention of preserving his life, avoiding injury to his body, and so on.   Whether he succeeded in compassing these things would, of course, now that he was a reasonable being, be a matter of indifference to him.   It would be enough that he had done his best to compass them.

In laying stress upon this natural connexion between certain objects of instinctive desire and the human animal, the Stoics were no doubt moved in great measure by the purpose of ruling out from the category of the ' natural ' altogether a great mass of the refinements and elaborations which went with civilized society.   The Cynic ideal of the simple life still worked in Stoicism.   Of course, if you rigidly apply the principle that everything in the accessories of human society which distinguishes it from the life of the animal horde is unnatural, you would make away with human society altogether, and no Stoic teacher, I think, did anything of the kind.   On the other hand, if you once allow, as the Stoics did, that in the society of reasonable beings many things are in place which are not natural on the merely animal level, you can only use the term ' natural ' intelligently, if you mean ' according to the norm which man ought to realize '.   The term gives us no light as to what that norm is.   Many people have felt that the life of complex societies, such as the Greek cities exhibited in the third century B.C.—though that was incomparably simpler than the life of our vast modern civilizations—prevents man from realizing the proper norm of his being as perfectly as he might under conditions nearer to those of primitive man or of the animals—the feeling which underlies the cry for the 'simple life'. If they are right, then they can say with justice that life without such and such complications is more 'natural' for man. People, however, who have this feeling have always been liable to use the word 'natural' in a double sense, the sense of 'what ought to be if man realizes his true being', and the other sense of 'near to primitive conditions', because the characteristics which civilized man shares with primitive man, and still more those which man shares with the beasts, are universal over a larger field and more 'natural' in that sense. By using the one word in this double sense they seem to prove that man realizes his true being the better, the nearer he is to primitive conditions. Of course, the proof of that is exactly what they beg by their use of the word.

The Stoics, among other advocates of the simple life, were open to this criticism. Yet they were right enough in feeling that among the things which made it difficult for the citizen of a Greek city, or the courtier of a Hellenistic king, to win the one good of inner peace and freedom were the complications of civilized society. He would never, for instance, have been distracted by the lust for gold, if the gold had been left where it was before, in the ground. To drag the precious metals out of the ground was therefore, they said, 'unnatural'. So, too, to navigate the seas for the purpose of bringing the products of one country into another was 'unnatural'. One can see, I think, that one of the main things which recommended the concept of Nature, of the natural, to the Stoic preacher was the weapon it gave him for striking freely at the things which held men back from the way of peace. When he directed the intention of his disciples in selective action to those things which were 'primary in the order of nature' the phrase had a strongly negative, as well as a positive, meaning.

The practical result of the Stoic ethical teaching, so far as we have followed it at present, was that the things which the action of the Wise Man was directed to secure would largely be the same as those pursued by the common man. The text-books give the list of 'promoted things' as being, in the sphere of the soul, cleverness, skill, intellectual progress, and the like; in the sphere of the body, life, health, strength, good condition, completeness of members, beauty; in the sphere of detached things, wealth, repute, gentle birth, and the like.[1] Certain things, however, which the common man pursued would not for the Wise Man be even in the class of things promoted; he would not lift

---

[1] Προηγμένα μὲν οὖν εἶναι ἃ καὶ ἀξίαν ἔχει, οἷον ἐπὶ μὲν τῶν ψυχικῶν εὐφυΐαν, τέχνην, προκοπὴν καὶ τὰ ὅμοια· ἐπὶ δὲ τῶν σωματικῶν ζωήν, ὑγίειαν, ῥώμην, εὐεξίαν, ἀρτιότητα, κάλλος· ἐπὶ δὲ τῶν ἐκτὸς πλοῦτον, δόξαν, εὐγένειαν καὶ τὰ ὅμοια. Diog. Laert. vii. 106 = Stoic. vet. fr., vol. iii, frag. 127.

It may be asked how a man's birth could be a matter of selection, although Heine, indeed, remarked that one could not be too careful in the choice of one's parents. I imagine that the Stoic might adduce a case in which the Wise Man, if his parentage was disputed, would take steps to prove that he was well-born.

a finger to secure them, and the Stoics, no doubt in intentional defiance of the rival Epicurean school, maintained that Pleasure was among these. Pleasure was one of the things indifferent in the double sense; it had not even such value as would direct the action of the Wise Man to obtaining it, where he could. Whether an action produced pleasure or pain, it would no more enter his head to consider than it would to speculate on the number of his hairs.[1] We must remember that by pleasure the Stoics meant, perhaps exclusively, agreeable bodily sensation; even with this restriction the doctrine is sufficiently severe. But where the Wise Man pursued the same object as the common man, his mind in pursuing it was quite different; he would pursue it because Nature indicated it as a right thing for him to have, with a complete absence of desire.

So far, the objects which we have mentioned as

---

[1] In Diog. Laert. vii. 102, Pleasure is classed among the προηγμένα. This is probably an oversight (see Bonhöffer, *Die Ethik des Stoikers Epictet*, p. 174). It does not appear in the lists of προηγμένα given by Diog. Laert. in § 106, and in Stobaeus, ecl. ii. 81, 11 f., Wachsmuth, we read: Οὔτε δὲ προηγμένα οὔτ' ἀποπροηγμένα περὶ ψυχὴν μὲν ... περὶ δὲ σῶμα λευκότητα καὶ μελανότητα καὶ χαροπότητα καὶ ἡδονὴν πᾶσαν καὶ πόνον καὶ εἴ τι ἄλλο τοιοῦτο. The stock examples to describe these absolutely indifferent things (καθάπαξ ἀδιάφορα), which not only do not excite desire or fear (even the προηγμένα and ἀποπροηγμένα are indifferent in that way) but do not even direct intention, are οἷον τὸ ἀρτίας ἔχειν ἐπὶ τῆς κεφαλῆς τρίχας ἢ περιττάς, ἢ τὸ προτεῖναι τὸν δάκτυλον ὡδὶ ἢ ὡδί, ἢ τὸ ἀνελέσθαι τι τῶν ἐμποδών, κάρφος ἢ φύλλον (*Stoic. vet. frag.*, vol. iii, frag. 118). Death, being an ἀποπροηγμένον, is not indifferent in this full sense. 'Non enim sic mors indifferens est, quomodo utrum capillos pares habeas' (Seneca, *Ep.* 82, 15). Pleasure, we are to understand, *is* indifferent in this way.

directing the Wise Man's action have all been objects to which he would address himself, with the purpose of acquiring them himself; we have dealt with actions which in a common man would be self-regarding. Did the *kathēkonta*, the actions appropriate to a human being, include altruistic ones? Having set the Wise Man in a position of magnificent detachment from the world's unrest, could Stoicism draw him forth again into contact with the multitude? Stoicism here reaches the most critical part of its task, and it is extraordinarily interesting to trace its procedure. The Stoic teachers affirmed that social service was above all else appropriate to the Wise Man. Once more they brought in the concept of Nature in order to establish the connexion between the Wise Man and unsaved humanity—of Nature, as the purposive Intelligence ordering the Universe. So far as Nature's Purpose can be discovered by the constitution of things, the will of the Wise Man will be adjusted in accordance with it. Now the constitution of things showed clearly, the Stoics said, that Nature had not intended the individual man to be an isolated unit, but a citizen of the great City which is the whole world, a member of the species in all of whom dwelt a particle of the Divine Reason. They pointed, and pointed with justice, to the significant fact that among the primary animal instincts was found the altruistic one which impelled the parent to sacrifice itself for its young. The sphere, however, within which the primary instinct restricted mutual help was a narrow one, the sphere of the family. With the development of Reason, the individual man came to see his solidarity with the whole human race. He recognized that Nature intended him to devote himself to the service of society at large, to sacrifice his life, if occasion arose, for his friend or his city or mankind.

Such social actions were eminently *kathēkonta*, appropriate, and the Stoic books, when they use the term, refer principally to these. There are many fine passages enforcing the obligations which lie upon man as the member of a community, or drawing a picture of the beneficent toil of the Wise Man in a distressful world. When therefore we find one who wrote with knowledge of these things, Charles Bigg, saying that the formula of the Stoic was barely 'My soul and God', whereas the formula of the Christian is 'My soul, my brother's soul, and God',[1] our first impulse is to bring up against him passages of that kind, which seem to state so emphatically the duty of the individual to concern himself with his brethen. But I believe, if we look closer, we shall see that Charles Bigg was right. The Wise Man was not to *concern* himself with his brethren— that is the point—he was only to serve them. Benevolence he was to have, as much of it as you can conceive ; but there was one thing he must not have, and that was love. Here too, if that inner tranquillity and freedom of his was to be kept safe through everything—here too, as when he was intending to acquire objects for himself, he must engage in action without desire. He must do everything which it is possible for him to do, shrink from no extreme of physical pain, in order to help, to comfort, to guide his fellow-men, but

[1] *The Church's Task under the Roman Empire*, Preface, p. xiv.

whether he succeeds or not must be a matter of pure
indifference to him. If he has done his best to help
you and failed, he will be perfectly satisfied with having
done his best. The fact that you are no better off for
his exertions will not matter to him at all. Pity, in the
sense of a painful emotion caused by the sight of other
men's suffering, is actually a vice. The most that can
be allowed when the Wise Man goes to console a
mourner, is that he should feign sympathy as a means of
attaining his object, but he must take care not to feel it.
He may sigh, Epictetus says,[1] provided the sigh does
not come from his heart. In the service of his fellow
men he must be prepared to sacrifice his health, to
sacrifice his possessions, to sacrifice his life ; but there
is one thing he must never sacrifice, his own eternal
calm.

People are liable to treat these doctrines of Stoicism
as a kind of gratuitous overstraining of the note for the
sake of effect. Those who wish to set Stoicism in a
favourable light would have us not judge it by these
occasional exaggerations of its principle. Professor
Arnold glides over them as lightly and quickly as he
can. After all, he says, the Stoics insisted that a man
should do all he could to relieve distress, and that came
practically to the same thing as if they allowed him to
be sorry for it. I am afraid my feelings in the matter
differ totally from Professor Arnold's ; to me, curiously,
it would make all the difference in the world, if, when
my friend sighed for my trouble, I thought he really
minded or not. I do not think that the Stoic doctrine,

[1] *Encheir.* 16 πρόσεχε μέντοι μὴ ἔσωθεν στενάξῃς.

forbidding sympathy and pity, forbidding what we understand by love, was a perversion of their principle : it seems to me the essential consequence of it, a consequence of immense practical importance—the keystone, as it were, of their system..

Of course, even in antiquity the Stoic casting-out of pity excited repugnance. It was the great stumbling-block of Stoicism in the department of Ethics. Something in the heart of men rose up against it. It is difficult for us to-day in Europe to take it as seriously meant. Our own ethical code has been fashioned under the influence of a different ideal, the Christian one, which makes the highest good, not tranquillity, but love. I do not mean to imply that Europe is Christian in any real sense ; I do not think it is ; yet its standards of things have been powerfully affected by the Christianity which has somehow gone on subsisting in its midst. But when we look outside Christendom, the Stoic conception of the supreme good appears to command wide acceptance. Although the human heart in ancient Greece recoiled from the pitiless conclusion to which Stoic thought carried its premisses, the premiss that the supreme good was *eudaimonia*, a state of inner satisfaction, of tranquillity, was not challenged. And when we extend our survey still farther over the world, we may see that if you take the mere area over which the ideal of ancient Greek thought is dominant, it is larger than Europe. In India also complete detachment from the world of Fear and Desire has been for multitudes the supreme goal of wisdom, and Buddhism has carried from India the ideal of Detachment to the great nations which it has penetrated farther East. The Bhagavad-gita[1] and the Buddhist scriptures present strange harmonies of language with the Stoic teaching ; here, too, we find a great deal about good action, with the proviso that such action must be unaccompanied with desire ; a great deal about benevolence, provided that there be no love.

I think it is important to realize that mankind has two different ideals before it ; and I do not see how the ideal of Detachment is compatible with the ideal of Love. If we choose one, we must forgo the other ; each ideal appears faulty when judged by the measure of the other. With the one goes to a large extent the intellect of ancient Greece and of India, with the other the Christian Church and the hearts of men, the *anima naturaliter Christiana*; for neither in Greece nor India nor China have the philosophers been the whole of the people—nor their philosophy the whole of the philosophers. There have been things tending to obscure this divergence between the two ideals. The language used by the Stoics or Buddhists about benevolence may often be taken to be inspired by the Christian ideal of Love. On the other hand, the Christian ideal has involved detachment from many things, from ' the cares of this world, and the deceitfulness of riches and the lusts of other things ', and much of the language used about this sort of detachment in Christian books may seem to point to the ideal of ancient Greece and India. The Stoic sage strenuously labouring to do good and indifferent whether good is done, sighing with his stricken friend, but not from the heart, is a figure serving well

[1] See Note at end of Lecture.

to bring home to us the difference. And we may see, I think, that the Stoics and sages of India could say no less without giving up their whole scheme. If the supreme end is tranquillity, of what use would it be to set the Wise Man's heart free from disturbance by cutting off the Fear and Desire which made him dependent upon outside things, if one immediately opened a hundred channels by which the world's pain and unrest could flow into his heart through the fibres, created by love and pity, connecting his heart with the fevered hearts of men all round? A hundred fibres!—one aperture would suffice to let in enough of the bitter surge to fill his heart full. Leave one small hole in a ship's side and you let in the sea. The Stoics, I think, saw with perfect truth that if you were going to allow any least entrance of love and pity into the breast, you admitted something whose measure you could not control, and might just as well give up the idea of inner tranquillity at once. Where love is, action cannot be without desire; the action of love has eminently regard to fruit, in the sense of some result beyond itself—the one thing that seems to matter is whether the loved person really is helped by your action. Of course you run the risk of frustrated desire and disappointment. The Stoic sage was never frustrated and never disappointed. Gethsemane, looked at from his point of view, was a signal break-down. The Christian's Ideal Figure could never be accepted by the Stoic as an example of his typical Wise Man.

It was cast up as a reproach against Stoicism by its opponents in antiquity that its Wise Man was an impossible Ideal. The Stoics admitted that he was as rare in the real world as the phoenix; Socrates, perhaps, and Diogenes had attained; or perhaps not even they. What made it worse was that the Stoics recognized no inferior degrees of wisdom; an ideal useful in practical life is one which can be in some measure, however imperfectly, realized; the Stoics' ideal could not be realized at all, except perfectly. The man a foot below the water, in their favourite illustration, is in a drowning condition just as much as the man a mile down. Supposing a man attained, he passed by an instantaneous transition into the state of salvation, the state of the Wise Man; thenceforth he possessed all good and every imaginable kind of virtue; every action he performed was perfect (a *katorthōma*, a complete achievement). Every one except the Wise Man, even he who had progressed so far as to be on the point of attainment, was concluded under one condemnation as foolish and bad. And since wisdom was attained so rarely, if ever, the whole of mankind are to be thought of as in this evil case. I think even in this doctrine we may see more than the pedantic desire to carry out a rigid scheme in defiance of common sense. That the Stoics held up an ideal never completely realized in any concrete man is hardly to be considered a fault at all. That they refused to allow a relative worth to imperfect achievement is a more serious charge. But it was really very difficult for them, with their premises, to do so. For the whole point of the ideal state, as they presented it, was its security, its freedom from fear; a single breach in that security, and its virtue was gone. We may revert to the figure of the ship : a hole one foot in diameter, if not stopped, renders it unseaworthy as truly as a hole ten feet or twenty feet in diameter. The only difference is, that it takes less time to make the ship with the smaller hole seaworthy. And the Stoics said that there was just this difference between one man and another. All alike came short of the Wise Man's security, but there were some for whom but comparatively little work would be necessary to bring them into a state of salvation. The faint shadow of a chance that you might some day attain, that alone made it worth while to enter upon the way of learning and discipline which led in that direction. Those who were called wise, in the common popular sense, the masters of philosophy—he himself, Chrysippus said—were men walking along that road ; they had not indeed attained wisdom, but they were 'advancing' (*prokoptontes*). I cannot help feeling that there was something fine in the persistent refusal of the Stoics to take any second-best instead of their Ideal, to say always to every actual character you might set before them, 'No, not that, not that ; the one we have dreamed of is fairer far than that, more magnificent and wonderful. Earth has never seen him, or at best it saw him but for a moment, and he was gone.'

It is said that when the Stoics came to practice they had to give up their impossible sages, and construct a scheme of duties for the common man, and it is sometimes said that the *kathēkonta*, 'appropriate things,' were these duties of a lower order which the Stoics had to teach, in default of the perfect actions (the *katorthōmata*) of the Wise Man. This, I think, is a confusing way of putting the case, and the translation of *kathēkonta* by our word 'duties' is unfortunate. The *kathēkonta* were the actions appropriate, according to the order of Nature, to every living being after its kind ; in the case of man the actions appropriate to his human character, described in their formal aspect. As performed by the Wise Man, they would be 'perfect *kathēkonta*' or '*katorthōmata*' because their inner content, the spirit in which they were performed, would be completely right. The *kathēkonta* can be performed by the common man—and will, of course, be performed by those who are *prokoptontes*, advancing—only in the sense that their action is the same as the Wise Man's, looked at from the outside ; it would not be a *katorthōma*, because the accompanying spiritual state will have been imperfect. We may think of Nature as the cosmic dramaturge, and the *kathēkonta* as the rôle she has attached to each character in the drama, only in this case the state of mind of each actor, as he plays his part, is as important as the formal correctness of his action. For instance, the action *Rendering back a deposit* is a *kathēkon* attached by Nature to the rôle of *Man* ; the common man can perform it so far as external correctness goes ; the Wise Man alone can perform it *phronimōs*, in the spirit of wisdom, and therefore make the action a good one in the true sense. The *kathēkonta* set before the common man are not a different set of duties, a different scheme of action, from those set before the sage ;[1] they are just the bare book

[1] As Professor W. L. Davidson (*The Stoic Creed*, p. 154) seems to suppose.

of the play, as it were, not in themselves good or bad, but neutral (*mesa*), becoming good only when filled with the spirit put into them by the Wise Man. Because even the common man can perform the letter of the drama, the *kathēkonta* are set before him also, and his performance of them will advance him that far on the way towards goodness. It is this fact which has misled the people who take them to be a lower order of duties framed by the Stoics as a concession to human weakness. There is no concession here, so far as I can see. In practice, no doubt, they habitually accommodated themselves to the ordinary view by treating a *kathēkon* performed by an unsaved man as a good action, but their theory of the *kathēkonta* does not seem to me to show any weakening in their dogma.

In a somewhat casual manner we have now walked about the city of refuge constructed in this troublous world by the prophet-philosophers of the Porch; we have told the towers thereof and marked the bulwarks. That fabric of dogma will seem to many grim and unpleasing. The very fact that dogma is beginning to take the place of the tentative speculation of earlier days will be pointed to as evidence that the Greek spirit is in decline. I think we must admit that from the point of view of the pure philosopher, the Stoic dogmatic system is on a lower level than the philosophy of Plato or Aristotle. The desire to know what is true, without any regard to the emotional value or practical consequences of what is discovered, is the only motive which should govern a philosopher, as a philosopher. And the Stoic philosophy was determined all through, we must admit, by a practical need. The pure philosopher is, however, an abstraction not embodied in any living man, and the desire to know for knowing's sake is not the only legitimate desire belonging to human nature. Few people would consider it immoral in any one whose friend was accused of something disgraceful, if he approached the examination of the facts with the wish to find one alternative true rather than the other. It is only required of him not to falsify what he finds. And why should it be immoral, when the Power governing the Universe is accused of being indifferent to Good and Evil, if a man approaches the momentous question with a wish to find one alternative true rather than the other? He will only be blameable, surely, if his wish induces him to falsify facts. The wish of the Stoics to ascertain that the Power governing the Universe was rational led them into a dogmatism, for which a modern man will probably consider they had no justification. He will feel that they ought to have spoken with more diffidence and hesitation on matters so far transcending human reach, or that they ought even to have suspended judgement altogether. I do not myself think that we are shut up to the alternative between Stoic dogmatism and the attitude of mere scepticism. The Stoic dogmatism was certainly a philosophic fall. I would only urge, in the Stoics' defence, that it is unfair to talk as if the world could stop still while we are ascertaining by pure philosophy of just how much we can be certain. Meanwhile, there is life to be lived. It was an immediately urgent problem for hundreds in the Athens of 300 B.C. on what principle, on what estimate of the world, they were going to frame their lives in that very moment of time. Stoicism gave them a scale of values, and I think we have good ground for believing that it did nerve innumerable men for centuries to brave action and brave endurance in a world where brute force and cruelty had dreadful scope. The philosopher's cloak, we may be sure, often covered a mass of human weakness and even villainy—so far mockers like Lucian had facts to bear out their bitter laughter. But there must have been true men, in order to make the Stoic a credible figure for so many centuries. We should have found, I think, could we have visited that old world, men of different ranks and conditions, free men and slaves, going through life with a strange tranquillity and strength—with that almost uncanny detachment still to-day, we are told, attained in countries where deliverance from Desire and Fear is taken as the supreme goal, and sought by the path of a long, deliberate discipline.

NOTE TO LECTURE II, p. 69

IT may be of interest to notice the affinity with Stoic doctrine in such passages of the Bhagavad-gita as the following. I take them from Mr. Barnett's translation in the 'Temple Classics'.

1. *The Stoic wise man has certainty of the truth and is never misled by sense-impressions.*

All works without limit, O son of Pritha, are contained in knowledge. . . . Knowing that, thou wilt never again fall into such bewilderment, O son of Pāṇḍu. . . Even though thou shouldst be of all sinners the greatest evil-doer, thou shalt be by the boat of knowledge carried over all evil. [*In Stoicism a man who attained passed by an instantaneous transition from the state of ignorance and misery to that of wisdom and bliss.*] . . . There is naught here that is like in power of cleansing to knowledge : this the adept of the Rule himself finds after many days in his Self. Knowledge he wins who has faith, who is devoted, who restrains the instruments of sense ; having won knowledge, he speedily comes to supreme peace (iv. 33–9).

That understanding, O son of Pritha, is of the Goodness-Mood, which knows action and inaction, the thing to be done and the thing to be not done, the thing to be feared and the thing to be not feared, bondage and deliverance (xviii. 30).

Cf. Πάλιν δὲ ὁριζόμενος αὐτῶν ἑκάστην (the virtues), τὴν μὲν ἀνδρείαν φησὶ φρόνησιν εἶναι ἐν ὑπομενετέοις· τὴν δὲ . . . φρόνησιν ἐν ἐνεργητέοις· τὴν δὲ δικαιοσύνην φρόνησιν ἐν ἀπονεμητέοις· Zeno, fr. 200, Arnim.

2. *Every one, except the Sage, is in a state of folly and misery, completely destitute of good.*

In him who is not under the Rule is no understanding; in him who is not under the Rule is no inspiration; in him who feels no inspiration peace is not ; in him who has not peace whence can there be joy ? (ii. 66).

3. *The action of the Sage is guided by the connexions established by Nature, τὰ καθήκοντα.*

For it was with works that Janaka and others came unto adeptship; thou too shouldst do them, considering the order of the world (iii. 20).

4. *But the action of the Sage is free from desire or attachment to any outside thing.*

As do the unwise, attached to works, O thou of Bharata's race, so should the wise do, but without attachment, seeking to establish order in the world (iii. 25).

Free from attachment to fruit of works, everlastingly contented, unconfined, even though he be engaged in work, he does not work at all (iv. 20).

Sacrifice, almsgiving, and mortification should not be surrendered, but should verily be done ; sacrifice, almsgiving, and mortification purify sages. But these very works must be done with surrender of attachment and fruits ; such is the decision of my most high doctrine, O son of Pṛithā (xviii. 5, 6). A worker is said to be of Goodness who is free from attachment, speaks not of an *I*, is possessed of constancy and vigour, and is unmoved whether he gain or gain not (xviii. 26).

In works be thine office ; in their fruits must it never be. Be not moved by the fruit of works; but let not attachment to worklessness dwell in thee. Abiding under the Rule and casting off attachment, O Wealth-Winner, so do thy works, indifferent alike whether thou gain or gain not. Indifference is called the Rule (ii. 47, 48).

5. *Hence the Sage is never afraid and never fails.*

Herein there is no failing of enterprise nor backsliding. Even a very little of this Law saves from the great dread (ii. 40).

6. *All things except the right state of his will are indifferent to him* (ἀδιάφορα).

The learned look with indifference alike upon a wise and courteous Brahman, a cow, an elephant, a dog, or an outcast man (v. 18). Most excellent is he whose understanding is indifferent alike to the friend, the lover, the enemy, the indifferent, the one facing both ways, the hateful, and the kinsman, alike to the good and the evil (vi. 9). One indifferent to foe and to friend, indifferent in honour and in dishonour, in heat and in cold, in joy and in pain, free of attachment, who holds in equal account blame and praise, silent, content with whatsoever befall, homeless, firm of judgement, possessed of devotion, is a man dear to Me (xii. 18. 19). Unattachment, independence of child, wife, home, and the like, everlasting indifference of mind whether fair or foul befall him . . . these are declared to be knowledge (xiii. 9, 10). He to whom pain and pleasure are alike ; who abides in himself; to whom clods, stones, or gold are alike ; to whom things sweet and things not sweet are equal ; who is wise ; to whom blame and praise of himself are equal; who is indifferent to honour and dishonour, indifferent to the interests of friend or foe ; who renounces all undertakings—he is said to have passed beyond the Moods (xiv. 24, 25).

7. *He is without emotions,* ἀπαθής.

He whose mind is undismayed in pain, who is freed from longings for pleasure, from whom passion, fear, and wrath have fled, is called a man of abiding prudence, a saintly man. He who is without affection for aught, and whatever fair or foul fortune may betide neither rejoices in it nor loathes it, has wisdom abidingly set (ii. 56, 57).   He who rejoices not, hates not, grieves not, desires not, who renounces alike fair and foul, and has devotion, is dear to Me (xii. 17).

8. *Love can find no place in his heart.*

He whom all loves enter as waters enter the full and immovably established ocean wins to peace ; not so the lover of loves (ii. 70).

The man whose every motion is void of love and purpose, whose works are burned away by the fire of Knowledge, the enlightened call 'learned' (iv. 19).   The learned grieve not for them whose lives are fled nor for them whose lives are not fled (ii. 11).

And so the Supreme Being declares of Himself :

'I am indifferent to all born beings ; there is none whom I hate, none whom I love' (ix. 29).

9. *The Sage is established in unshakeable calm and harmony with the Universe.*

When thine understanding, that erstwhile swayed unbalanced by reason of what thou hast heard, shall stand firm and moveless in concent, then shalt thou come into the Rule (ii. 53).   Firm of understanding, unbewildered, the knower of Brahma, who abides in Brahma, will not rejoice when pleasant things befall nor be dismayed when things unpleasing betide him.   His spirit unattached to outward touch, he finds in his Self pleasantness; his spirit following the Brahma-Rule, he is fed with undying pleasantness (*the Stoic* εὐπάθεια) (v. 20, 21).

10. *And yet certain involuntary bodily reactions remain even in the Sage* (Seneca, *De ira*, ii. 2, 3 ; *Epist.* 57. 3 ; 71, 29 ; 74, 31).

The ranges of sense vanish away from a body-dweller who haunts them not, save only relish (*rasa*) (ii. 59).

11. *No action of the Sage is haphazard, but every one part of a reasonable scheme of life.*

The sorrow-staying Rule is with him whose eating and walking are by rule, whose action in works is by rule, whose sleeping and waking are by rule (vi. 17).

12. *Deliverance is only won by a long and persevering discipline (ἄσκησις)*

Doubtless the mind is ill to check and fickle, O mighty-armed one ; but by constant labour and passionlessness, O son of Kuntī, it may be held. For one of unrestrained spirit the Rule is hard of attainment, I trow; but by one of obedient spirit who strives it may be won by the means thereto (vi. 35, 36).

It can hardly be necessary to point out that the headings (in italics) of the sections above are not part of the quotations, but give the Stoic doctrine to which the quotations show a parallel. Any one who went through Epictetus, Seneca, and Marcus Aurelius with the object of finding parallels to these extracts from the most popular devotional book of the Hindus could, I believe, find many striking similarities of phrase. One must, of course, admit that there is a great deal besides in the *Gita*, which belongs to a different world from that of the Stoics, and that the metaphysics and devotional religion which underly its ethics are different from the metaphysical basis of Stoicism. It is recognized, too, that the *Gita* is itself composed of heterogeneous elements, whether that is to be accounted for by the supposition that different hands in different centuries have been at work upon it (the view of Hopkins and Richard Garbe) or by the supposition that different streams of tradition had become confused in the mind of one author (as Mr. Barnett seems to believe). Passages, no doubt, may be found in the *Gita* inconsistent with the ruling out of love and emotion, which is exemplified in the passages cited above, and is logically required by the ideal of tranquillity.

LECTURE III

POSIDONIUS

LECTURE III

POSIDONIUS

If you read the literature which has accumulated in recent years about the religious and philosophical beliefs prevalent in the Greco-Roman world at the time of Christ, there is one personality whom you encounter at every turn, Posidonius. You gather that he is the one man whose mind penetrates and informs all the philosophical writing which has come down to us from that age. And yet till recently Posidonius was not a person who bulked very large in the thought of the average classical scholar. The fragments of which he is expressly stated in our sources to be the author do not, when collected, make a large book.[1] The late Master of Balliol published two volumes on *The Evolution of Theology in the Greek Philosophers* without mentioning the name of Posidonius. But the scholars who have worked in this field have come to believe that Posidonius is only very inadequately represented by the fragments expressly attributed to him. They have come to see Posidonius behind a great deal of Cicero, a great deal of Philo of Alexandria, of Diodorus, of Manilius, of Seneca, of Plutarch. We

[1] *Posidonii Rhodii reliquiae doctrinae, collegit atque illustravit Ianus Bake*, Lugduni-Batavorum, 1810. There is no more recent collection of the fragments.

may compare him perhaps to a painter of whose own work little is left, but whose style shines reflected in a whole school of pupils. So behind the later philosophical literature of antiquity stands, we are told, one great figure. Who was this man?

His original home was in Syria, at Apamea, one of the Greek cities founded, about a century and a half before his birth, on the Orontes. The place seems to have a more tropical character than most of Syria, a hot, swampy basin, shut in by hills, where the Seleucid kings had kept their herd of Indian elephants. Whether Posidonius had any native Syrian blood we do not know. At the time when he was born, about 135 B.C. apparently, the Seleucid kingdom was nearing its disruption. Posidonius was probably a child when the last strong king, Antiochus Sidetes, perished in his attempt to win back the Eastern provinces from the Parthian. After that, anarchy in Syria went from bad to worse. The princes of the royal house turned practically into *condottieri*, ranging the country with hired troops, in endless feuds, one against the other, and the cities, becoming more and more independent, carried on petty wars against each other on their own account. It was among such surroundings that Posidonius, we must suppose, grew up. Among the fragments of his writings are two which express his contemptuous disgust with the slack, pleasure-loving existence characteristic of the Syrian Greek cities, and the wretched farce of their military operations.[1] He

---

[1] Ποσειδώνιος δ' ἐκκαιδεκάτῃ Ἱστοριῶν περὶ τῶν κατὰ τὴν Συρίαν πόλεων λέγων ὡς ἐτρύφων γράφει καὶ ταῦτα· Τῶν γοῦν ἐν ταῖς πόλεσιν

must have left his country as quite a young man, if it is true that he sat under Panaetius at Athens. Panaetius of Rhodes, the friend of Scipio Aemilianus, in his old age presided in Athens over the Stoic School; and since he died about 110 B.C., Posidonius cannot have been at that date more than about twenty-five. Those were the days when Hasdrubal-Clitomachus, of whom we shall speak in the fourth lecture, was expounding the Scepticism of Carneades at Athens in the seat of Plato. Stoicism, however, was the teaching which the young Syrian Greek found to meet best the need of his heart, whether because his childhood in Syria had been under the influence of some indigenous mystical tradition, to which Stoic pantheism showed affinities, or because in his recoil from the baseness and frivolity of his home he was attracted by what was most earnest

ἀνθρώπων, διὰ τὴν εὐβοσίαν τῆς χώρας ἀπούσης [MSS. ἀπὸ] τῆς περὶ τὰ ἀναγκαῖα κακοπαθείας, συνόδους νεμόντων πλείονας, ἐν αἷς εὐωχοῦντο συνεχῶς, τοῖς μὲν γυμνασίοις ὡς βαλανείοις χρώμενοι, ἀλειφόμενοι δ' ἐλαίῳ πολυτελεῖ καὶ μύροις· τοῖς δὲ γραμματείοις—οὕτως γὰρ ἐκάλουν τὰ κοινὰ τῶν συνδείπνων—ὡς οἰκητηρίοις ἐνδιαιτώμενοι, καὶ τὸ πλεῖον τῆς ἡμέρας γαστριζόμενοι ἐν αὐτοῖς οἴνοις καὶ βρώμασιν, ὥστε καὶ προσαποφέρειν πολλὰ καὶ καταυλουμένους πρὸς χελιδόνος πολυκρότου ψόφον, ὥστε τὰς πόλεις ὅλας τοιούτοις κελάδοις συνηχεῖσθαι.   Athen. xii. 527 e f = Frag. Hist. Graec. iii. 258.

Ποσειδώνιος δ' ὁ ἀπὸ τῆς στοᾶς φιλόσοφος ἐν τῇ τρίτῃ τῶν Ἱστοριῶν διηγούμενος περὶ τῶν Ἀπαμέων πρὸς Λαρισαίους πολέμου γράφει τάδε· Παραζωνίδια καὶ λογχάρι' ἀνειληφότες ἰῷ καὶ ῥύπῳ κεκρυμμένα, πετάσια δ' ἐπιτεθειμένοι καὶ προσκόπια σκιὰν μὲν ποιοῦντα, καταπνεῖσθαι δ' οὐ κωλύοντα τοὺς τραχήλους, ὄνους ἐφελκόμενοι γέμοντας οἴνου καὶ βρωμάτωνπαντοδαπῶν, οἷς παρέκειτο φωτίγγια καὶ μοναύλια, κώμων οὐ πολέμων ὄργανα.   Athen. iv. 176 b = Frag. Hist. Graec. iii. 253.

and austere. All one can say is that, from the time he
was a young man, he seems to have turned his back
on the country of his birth: this does not look as if,
consciously at any rate, he wished to identify himself
with Syrian Hellenism. His face was towards the
West. All the lands round the Mediterranean had
just been brought together in a new way by the
unifying power of the republic on the Tiber, in process
of becoming an empire. And the curiosity of Posidonius
extended over all this realm. He saw with his own
eyes the sun set in the Atlantic beyond the verge of
the known world,[1] and the African coast over against
Spain, where the trees were full of apes,[2] and the villages
of barbarous peoples inland from Marseilles, where
human heads hanging at the house-doors for trophies
were an everyday sight.[3] When at last, about 95 B.C.,
he wanted to fix his home somewhere, he chose the place
where, perhaps more than any other, the old Greek

---

[1] Λέγειν γὰρ δή φησι Ποσειδώνιος τοὺς πολλοὺς μείζω δύνειν τὸν
ἥλιον ἐν τῷ παρωκεανίτιδι καὶ μετὰ ψόφου παραπλησίως ὡσανεὶ
σίζοντος τοῦ πελάγους κατὰ σβέσιν αὐτοῦ διὰ τὸ ἐμπίπτειν εἰς τὸν
βυθόν . . . τὸ δὲ ψεῦδος ἐλέγξαι φησὶ τριάκονθ᾽ ἡμέρας διατρίψας ἐν
Γαδείροις καὶ τηρήσας τὰς δύσεις. Strabo iii. 1. 5, C. 138.

[2] Πιθήκων . . . περὶ ὧν καὶ Ποσειδώνιος εἴρηκεν ὅτι πλέων ἐκ Γαδείρων
εἰς τὴν Ἰταλίαν προσενεχθείη τῇ Λιβυκῇ παραλίᾳ καὶ ἴδοι τῶν θηρίων
μεστόν τινα τούτων ἁλιτενῆ δρυμόν, τῶν μὲν ἐπὶ τοῖς δένδρεσι τῶν δ᾽
ἐπὶ γῆς, ἐχόντων ἐνίων καὶ σκύμνους καὶ ἐπεχόντων μαστόν· γελᾶν
οὖν ὁρῶν βαρυμάστους, ἐνίους δὲ φαλακρούς, τοὺς δὲ κηλήτας καὶ ἄλλα
τοιαῦτα ἐπιφαίνοντας σίνη. id. xviii. 3. 4, C. 827.

[3] Φησὶ γοῦν Ποσειδώνιος αὐτὸς ἰδεῖν ταύτην τὴν θέαν πολλαχοῦ, καὶ
τὸ μὲν πρῶτον ἀηθίζεσθαι, μετὰ δὲ ταῦτα φέρειν πρᾴως διὰ τὴν συνήθειαν.
id. iv. 4. 5, C. 198.

republican spirit still survived, a strenuous maritime state, as great a contrast to the cities of Syria as any Greek city could be, the city of his Stoic master Panaetius. Posidonius became a citizen by adoption of Rhodes. Among this free people he spent the second half of his long life. Once he held the highest office in the state, the *prytany*. At another time he went as ambassador for Rhodes to Rome. His name, before he died, was become well known all over the Greek world; in those circles of Roman society where interest in Greek literature and Greek thought was alive, he had many personal friends. Cicero, in his young days, spent some time in Rhodes in order to study Greek philosophy under him, and they continued in later life to correspond. In 59 Cicero sent his own account of his consulship to his old master, suggesting that he, the most eminent Greek historian of the day, might find it fit matter for his pen—a suggestion which unfortunately fell flat. On two occasions, it would seem, Pompey, during his wars in the East, turned aside to visit the philosopher of Rhodes. The death of Posidonius fell apparently about 51 B.C., when he had reached the ripe age of 84.

It is not only as a philosopher in the special sense that Posidonius stood at the head of his generation. His historical work, continuing Polybius, is the great source from which our notices of the Greek East in that period, in Strabo or Diodorus or Plutarch, are derived. Posidonius, as a historian, is however a subject which belongs to another inquiry. Here one may only observe, looking at the fragments of his history which have come down

to us, how predominantly his concern as a moral philosopher seems to have directed his attention to anthropo-
logy and to ethical values.   He expatiated with curious
interest upon the manners and customs of peoples like
the Kelts of the Far West.[1]   Instances of luxury or
moral weakness it was his way to set in the fierce light
of a minute description ;[2] on the other hand, he recorded
with obvious satisfaction, how the peoples of Italy were
still so frugal that even well-to-do people expected their
sons to dine happily on nuts or pears and drink nothing
but water.[3]   With regard to moral standards, at any rate,
the traditions of his Syrian home had worked upon him
mainly in the way of antipathy.

Besides occupying a conspicuous place in the roll of
Greek historians, Posidonius meets us again as a notable
figure when we come into the field of Natural Science in
antiquity.   His extensive travels towards the North and
West were largely prompted by the desire to make scientific observations of tides and physical phenomena generally, and in this department, too, he delivered his results
to the world in a voluminous series of writings.   Something of all that still reaches us through the medium of
Strabo, or Seneca in his *Natural Questions*, and passed
on through later writers into the tradition of the Middle
Ages.   But again it would belong to a special inquiry,

---

[1] Πολλὰ παρὰ πολλοῖς ἔθιμα καὶ νόμιμα ἀναγράφων.   Athen. iv.
151 e.

[2] See, for instance, the description of the Syrian towns already
alluded to ; of Damophilus, the Sicilian slave-master, himself the ' slave
of soft living ' τρυφῆς δοῦλος, frag. 15 ; of the feasts of King Antiochus
Sidetes, frag. 17 ; &c. (*Frag. Hist. Graec.*).

[3] Frag. 3 (*Frag. Hist. Graec.*).

which is outside the purpose of these lectures, to study the significance of Posidonius as a man of science. It is in his character of philosopher and theologian that he comes within our purview.

And the first thing, I think, which is obvious about Posidonius when we look at him in this respect, is that he represents a tendency which had come to prevail largely in the time preceding the Christian era—the tendency of the different schools of Greek philosophy to coalesce. Eclecticism, syncretism, was, we know, the note of religious and philosophical thought in the later stages of the ancient paganism. The Sceptical and the Epicurean schools, of course, stood out, and maintained a hostile attitude to the rest, so far as they managed to survive. But the atmosphere of the time was unfavourable to them. Among men of leisure and elegant interests, Epicureanism still had numerous adherents in the last century B. c., but in a generation or two it had dwindled to be an eccentric creed under popular reprobation. On the other hand, the philosophies which stood for ideal values against all scepticism and materialism, whether of the philosophic or of the popular kind, felt more and more that they were upholding a common cause and drew together. The school of Plato, as represented by the men actually in occupation of the Academy, when Posidonius was a young man in Athens, had, as we shall see, settled altogether into the sceptical line, but the writings of Plato himself, with all they contained of positive doctrine, the writings of his early disciples, Xenocrates and Philip of Opus, were still there. The Pythagorean writings, too, with which the positive side of Plato and the older Academy had had such close affinity, were still there. In the Peripatetic school a theory of the world and human conduct was still maintained which, if not quite of a pattern that the strict Stoics could approve, agreed at any rate with them in maintaining that the Reason in man was akin to the Divine principle at work in the Universe, and that no good could be set in the scale against virtue. At a time when many men, not philosophers in any special sense, wanted some guide for life which was raised above the old mythologies and which yet met their sense of some greater spiritual Reality encompassing the life of men, it was natural that a kind of body of popular philosophic doctrine should come into vogue, made of the commonplaces of the different schools, with a blurring of their distinctive peculiarities. People got the idea of a sort of common philosophic stuff at the back of the differences, very much, I think, as a large number of people of to-day cling to the idea of something which they call 'undenominational', 'undogmatic' religion—the idea of some common religious stuff which you may take for granted at the back of all articulate religious beliefs. I suppose you are bound to get this sort of popular eclecticism wherever there is a widespread craving for positive theory of some kind, and the multitude is confronted with a variety of teachers. The multitude has not the ability or the patience to think out the issues, and some theory it must have, so it takes what it wants from any quarter and makes its own compound as best it can, in its own muddled happy-go-lucky way. The eclecticism of later antiquity was the inevitable consequence of philosophy becoming popular.

It may be, of course, that in certain cases the multitude is right, that the instinct which guides its casual selection and rejection is on the whole sound.   In such cases we may expect that if a great independent thinker arises, he too will take elements impartially from the different rival systems and combine them in a new body. But it will be a new *body*, a new system with an organic life of its own, not a mere aggregate of diverse elements, like the philosophy of the multitude.   Teachers, however, of another kind may arise.   The philosophic schools are not above being influenced by the conditions in the world round about them.   When eclecticism is in the air, a philosopher, who is not a great original thinker, may dominate his age simply by putting together the different elements which the age wants—which he himself, as a child of the age, wants—in the proper philosophic dress, in an effective literary shape.   Did the last century before Christ produce any great thinker, to take up the tradition of the different schools, and give the world a new system, stamped with his own creative originality, like the systems of Plato and Aristotle generations before, and the systems of Plotinus and Augustine generations later?   Or did it only produce teachers able to give philosophic shape to the popular eclecticism?

Of all its philosophic writers, only two survive in their own works to-day—the Italian Cicero and the Hebrew Philo, if we may be allowed to reckon Philo to this century, since he can hardly have been more than thirty at the birth of Christ.   Now Cicero is eminently a type of the writer who gives effective literary shape to other people's thought, and the philosophy which Philo expounds is essentially the popular Greek philosophy, a blend of Platonism, Pythagoreanism, and Stoicism, slightly modified by the Hebrew belief in God. But behind the Italian and behind the Hebrew are their Greek teachers, whom we know only through them and through later writers, and amongst those teachers the figure of Posidonius bulks most largely. Do we discern in that background any great work of fresh constructive thought ?

I don't think we do. I don't think either Posidonius, or Antiochus of Ascalon, who made his own blend of Platonism and Stoicism, or any other Greek teacher of the time that we know of, can count for much as an original thinker. There is no distinctive philosophy of Posidonius as there is a distinctive philosophy of Plato or Plotinus. The importance of Posidonius does not lie there. It was rather his great work, that no one else gathered up so completely the mass of beliefs which held the minds of men and gave them a form so impressive and eloquent as he did. The great body of his writings expressed with unique completeness the general mind of the Greek world at the Christian era : he focused it and made it conscious of itself. Hence it was that later writers on theology and philosophy, on geography and natural science, found Posidonius the most productive and most readily accessible source to draw from. He combined the advantages of a highly-coloured and fascinating writer [1] with those of an encyclopaedia.

---

[1] Ποσειδώνιος δὲ τὸ πλῆθος τῶν μετάλλων ἐπαινῶν καὶ τὴν ἀρετὴν

The fact, of course, that the matter of Posidonius was drawn from the stock philosophy of the schools and from popular belief makes it harder to assign to him personally with any security much that we find in later writers of the same character. For it may have come to them through other mediums. It has been pointed out, for instance, that the philosophy taken over from the Greeks by Philo of Alexandria is very much the same sort of blend of Platonism and Stoicism as seems to have been retailed by Posidonius. It is unlikely that Philo did his own compounding. Hence, the German, keen ever to discover sources behind sources, cries 'Posidonius' jubilantly.[1] Now, although Philo never mentions the name of Posidonius, it may well be that the writings of that philosopher were actually the chief source from which he drew. But for the reason I have pointed out, this seems to me just a case where we cannot be sure. We are apt to forget that the great names of antiquity which have come down to us were associated in the real world with thousands of little names now forgotten; that all over the Greek world, when Philo wrote, there were hundreds of schools humming with the old commonplaces, and hundreds of eager scribblers putting down the old themes with some slight novelty of variation—think of Horace's Crispinus, inexhaustibly

οὐκ ἀπέχεται τῆς συνήθους ῥητορείας, ἀλλὰ συνενθουσιᾷ ταῖς ὑπερβολαῖς. Strabo iii. 2. 9, C. 147. See Norden, *Die antike Kunstprosa*, p. 154, note.

[1] In this case a German lady. See Mathilda Apelt, ' De rationibus quibusdam quae Philoni Alexandrino cum Posidonio intercedunt', in *Commentationes Philologae Jenenses*, vol. iii, fasc. i, 1907—an interesting conspectus of points in which Philo coincides with the Posidonian body of ideas.

prolific of little books of popular Stoicism ; we are apt to forget how much of the propagation, transmission, modification of ideas must have been performed by that obscure, unrecorded industry, which no *Quellenkritik* will ever be able to trace.

The consolation is, that the very circumstances which make it difficult to identify the work of Posidonius in other writers make it less important to do so. If the real significance of Posidonius is that he focused and expressed the general belief of his time, the important thing is the general belief itself. And this we can extract with assurance from the documents. We can see a certain common element running through much of Cicero and Seneca and Plutarch and Philo of Alexandria—a body of ideas whose general currency they presuppose. If we like to label this body of ideas ' Posidonius ', in order to give it a distinctive name, it may be useful to do so. What really matters is, that we should grasp the body of ideas as a fact of the world at that period of time.

Stoicism, as we saw in previous lectures, with its dogmatic formulae and its categorical rules of conduct, was fitted more than any other philosophy to take the place of decaying religion in the ordinary educated society of the Greco-Roman world. And Stoicism was the basis of the body of ideas represented by Posidonius. But Stoicism of the high-and-dry scholastic kind, although it purported to give men the key of the universe and human life, left many of their natural desires unsatisfied. It did not tell them all they wanted to know. It did not completely make them feel at home in the Universe. In order to do that, it would have to give them more than a hard abstract scheme ; it would have to fill in the detail in a way which would give the imagination something to cleave to. Supposing, for instance, you held the view, sanctioned by Cleanthes and Chrysippus, that the good man's soul maintained its individual existence after death till it was re-absorbed into the Primal Fire, you had not, I suppose, any very clear image before your mind of a destiny to be desired. And this kind of defect was, one must believe, more generally felt at the time of the Christian era than in the days when Stoicism was first instituted. For some reason or other, men apparently had come to feel more keenly the inadequacy of a life limited by our bodily senses, to strain more and more, in tedium or disgust, or in some craving for a larger life, away from this world to the Unexplored beyond. Of course, the feeling had always existed to some extent : the old Bacchic and Orphic sects centuries before had borne witness to it among the Greeks : but in the later world the feeling had become more general. This is one of those shiftings of mood which come in the life of peoples as well as in that of individuals, hard to account for, except partially, hard often to grasp with any precision. A feeling came over men, and suddenly the familiar Universe seemed a strange place, terrifying in its enormous magnitude— the earth stretching into regions of unexplored possibilities, moved and shaken by inhuman forces, and over all the silent enigma of the wheeling stars. They awoke, as it were, to find themselves lost in the streets

of a huge, strange city. The old Stoicism was inadequate
to meet the needs of a mood like that.

To make men at home in the Universe—it seems to
me that perhaps such a formula as that would give the
key to the whole activity of Posidonius, his work in
geography and physics and history as well as in philosophy. If you had read through the mass of his writings, you might really look round upon this world and
know where you were. You would have some definite
image of the shape of the earth upon which you stood,
and things like tides and earthquakes would no longer
be the manifestation of some utterly unknown power.
And especially when you looked up to the sky and the
shining bodies which moved about there, some with
such impressive regularity, some appearing and dis-
appearing at odd moments, you would have some
notion what it all meant. But it would be quite
insufficient for peace of mind that a man should know
merely the shape and mechanism of the house in which
he found himself. It was still more important to know
who his fellow denizens were, to know what it meant
for him when the body which was the organ of his
conscious life was left a dead and empty shell. And as
to these things there were actually in circulation, come
down from former generations, a number of positive
statements. It is impossible for us now to know how
far the ideas thrown out by Plato in his vivid myths as
to the soul's destinies, how far the doctrines of the
Orphics and Pythagoreans, actually commanded belief
among average educated Greeks at a time when the
official heads of the Platonic society had lapsed into

Scepticism.   We only know that the writings of Plato himself were still widely read, and the books of the Pythagoreans and older Academics were still accessible. We may be sure that the ideas they suggested were still a living issue, that the minds of many men dwelt upon them, wondering whether they were true.   You may remember that a contemporary of Posidonius, a fellow Stoic, the Roman Cato, spent the evening before his suicide in re-reading the *Phaedo*.   How many people beside Posidonius eked out Stoicism by drawing upon this body of ideas we do not know.   We know that this is just what Posidonius did.   We know, too, that just at the same time there was a new outburst of Pythagoreanism, in which Cicero's friend Nigidius Figulus was prominent.

But the kind of ideas as to the soul and its destinies which we find in the Orphics and Pythagoreans and Plato had not been an independent creation of some Greek visionaries centuries before.   It seems to me that O. Gruppe does good service when he insists, in his book on Greek religion, that the appearance of such doctrines among the Greeks was only part of a larger movement—a 'mystical' movement, Gruppe calls it, and though the term is open to misunderstanding I don't know any better one to suggest—which affected the peoples of Nearer Asia as well as the Greeks in the sixth century B.C.[1]   In consequence of this movement, we may believe that ideas were still current, were in the air, among great masses of mankind at the time of Posidonius, which we can only very imperfectly trace in

[1] Gruppe, *Griechische Mythologie*, § 287.

our existing literary documents. Posidonius, on this view, in combining Stoicism with Platonic doctrine as to the soul and its destinies was accommodating philosophy to a great body of popular belief.

But Stoicism could not be combined with Platonism and not suffer some modifications in its structure. A characteristic running through the mystical doctrines—popular, Pythagorean, Platonic—was the strongly-marked dualism of body and soul. 'The body a tomb' (*sōma*—*sēma*) was everywhere its key-note. The basis of the conviction was no doubt a real experience; there did actually sometimes come over men with compelling power a feeling of the essential inadequacy of the sense-life, dissatisfaction with all that the senses could supply to the understanding, still more poignant dissatisfaction with all that the senses could supply in passionate pleasure to the emotions. And such feeling was met by the assertion that there dwelt verily in this body a Being of immortal nature that yearned for the radiant sphere whence it had come. No wonder it found the body narrow and fetid and dark! In one form or other that had been said by the Orphics and Pythagoreans, by Empedocles and Plato.

But Stoicism in its original form had strictly ruled out this dualism. The body was of the same substance, in a depotentiated state, as the soul. The antithesis for the orthodox Stoics was not between body and soul, but between emotion (*pathos*) and tranquillity. Wherever the dualism prevailed, the bodily appetites were especially what was pointed at when one spoke of the body prevailing over the soul. Sin tended to become nothing more and nothing less than the surrender of the soul to bodily appetites, and on the other hand the redemption of the soul consisted essentially in resisting or suppressing these appetites; an ascetic discipline of life was the natural corollary of the dualistic view in the sphere of conduct. But yet it was obvious to thought that these appetites and passions were not outside the soul but within it; they were a part of consciousness; if a man was greedy, it was not that his material body compelled his soul to its own separate will, but that the man chose certain sorts of consciousness in preference to other sorts.

It had seemed to Plato that the psychological facts were best represented, as you well know, by depicting the Soul as a combination of three entities—the Reason, the Part you are angry with, and the Part which feels appetite. His pictorial representation did obviously serve well to describe some aspects of experience, the way in which different selves seem to be fighting with each other for dominance in what we call conflicts of Reason and Passion. On the other hand, if you took Plato's description literally, you were brought up against the fact that after all it was one self which reasoned and desired, one self which ultimately chose this or that sort of consciousness. The Stoics—at any rate Chrysippus, for the views of Zeno and his first disciples on the point seem doubtful—felt strongly the unity of the agent as against Plato's threefold division. Chrysippus insisted that only one Ruling Principle, one *hēgemonikon*, was concerned, which itself underwent a modification for evil, when it turned from what was

reasonable to inordinate emotion: an irrational part of
the soul, he said, such as Plato had supposed, was a
figment. The Ruling Principle in man was Reason all
through: the passions were diseases of the Reason
itself: they were wrong judgements of value.

Our first thought might be that such a view of the
soul, insisting on its unity, lent itself better to the
dualistic tendency than the Platonic view, especially
when coupled, as by the Stoics, with the theory that the
reason in each man was a fragment of the One Divine
Fire. But on second thoughts we see, I think, that if
it was the feeling of the nobler part of them being
overmastered by an alien power which really drove men
to the dualism of Soul and Body, the Stoic theory
which recognized no alien power in the constitution of
man would not do. Stoicism did, of course, distinguish
the Reason, the spark of Divine Fire, from the body of
gross flesh, but by bringing the passions within the
Reason it made the division in the wrong place from
the Orphic, Pythagorean, Platonic point of view.
There must be a root of evil in man himself, a law in
his members warring against the law of his mind, and
this was given by the irrational part of the soul in the
Platonic psychology. Posidonius, on this point, set
himself emphatically on the side of Plato against the
orthodox Stoic tradition. He wrote a special work in
several books, *Concerning the Passions*, against Chrysippus, considerable fragments of which have been
excavated from Galen.[1] He attacked the view that the

---

[1] Mainly from the treatise Περὶ τῶν καθ᾽ Ἱπποκράτην καὶ Πλάτωνα

passions were simply wrong judgements of the Reason.
If so, how was it that they lost their power, wore themselves out, with time? No one got tired of believing
that twice two was four. Yes, 'the cause of the
passions,' he writes in a fragment which Galen probably
gives word for word, 'the cause, that is, of disharmony
and the unhappy life, is that men do not follow
absolutely the *daimōn* that is in them, which is akin to,
and has a like nature with, the Power governing the whole
kosmos, but turn aside after the lower animal principle
and let it run away with them. Those who fail to see
this . . . do not perceive that the first point in happiness is to be led in nothing by the irrational, unhappy,
godless element in the soul.' [1] The figure of Reason as
the charioteer controlling, or failing to control, the
irrational parts of the soul—that figure, suggested by
Plato, is the one that sums up the Psychology and
Ethics, to which the bulk of the educated world sub-
scribed at the time of the Christian era. Posidonius
uses it, of course: Philo recurs to it again and again.
In one passage the language of Posidonius takes a more

δογμάτων: see M. Pohlenz, *De Posidonii libris περὶ παθῶν* in the
Jahrbücher für classische Philologie, Supplementband xxiv, 1898.

[1] Τὸ δὴ τῶν παθῶν αἴτιον, τουτέστι τῆς τε ἀνομολογίας καὶ τοῦ
κακοδαίμονος βίου τὸ μὴ κατὰ πᾶν ἕπεσθαι τῷ ἐν αὑτοῖς δαίμονι
συγγενεῖ τε ὄντι καὶ τὴν ὁμοίαν φύσιν ἔχοντι τῷ τὸν ὅλον κόσμον
διοικοῦντι, τῷ δὲ χείρονι καὶ ζῳώδει ποτὲ συνεκκλίνοντας φέρεσθαι. οἱ
δὲ τοῦτο παριδόντες οὔτε ἐν τούτοις βελτιοῦσι τὴν αἰτίαν τῶν παθῶν
οὔτε ἐν τοῖς περὶ τῆς εὐδαιμονίας καὶ ὁμολογίας ὀρθοδοξοῦσιν· οὐ γὰρ
βλέπουσιν, ὅτι πρῶτόν ἐστιν ἐν αὐτῇ τὸ κατὰ μηδὲν ἄγεσθαι ὑπὸ τοῦ
ἀλόγου τε καὶ κακοδαίμονος καὶ ἀθέου τῆς ψυχῆς. Pohlenz, *De
Posidonii libris περὶ παθῶν*, p. 625.

urgent note.   We hear the cry which was going up
from the hearts of many men in that old world for
deliverance from something in themselves.   Chrysippus
and the orthodox Stoics maintained that there was no
root of evil in human nature, and they explained moral
evil in each individual, somewhat naively, as due to the
bad influences of society.   But Posidonius, says Galen,
does not hold that badness enters into men from without only and has no root of its own in our souls.
'The germ of badness is in ourselves, and what we all
need is not so much to run away from the wicked as to
follow after those who may make us clean and hinder
the badness from growing in us.'[1]   'The irrational,
unhappy, godless element of the soul'—a hundred
years later some one was crying 'Wretched man that I
am, who shall deliver me from the body of this death?'

The books of the old Academy and the Pythagoreans,
where Posidonius found this doctrine of the soul, had also
a good deal to say about the destinies of the soul, when
it did escape from the prison of the body.   Here too
he, and the popular philosophy, filled up the deficiencies
of scholastic Stoicism,—and that although his master
Panaetius had departed from the tradition in the contrary
direction, not by elaborating the picture of life after
death, but by denying the survival of the individual

---

[1] Οὐ τοίνυν οὐδὲ Ποσειδωνίῳ δοκεῖ τὴν κακίαν ἔξωθεν ἐπεισιέναι τοῖς
ἀνθρώποις οὐδεμίαν ἔχουσαν ἰδίαν ῥίζαν ἐν ταῖς ψυχαῖς ἡμῶν, ὅθεν
ὁρμωμένη βλαστάνει τε καὶ αὐξάνεται, ἀλλ' αὐτὸ τοὐναντίον. καὶ γὰρ
οὖν καὶ τῆς κακίας ἐν ἡμῖν αὐτοῖς σπέρμα. καὶ δεόμεθα πάντες οὐχ οὕτω
τοῦ φεύγειν τοὺς πονηροὺς ὡς τοῦ διώκειν τοὺς καθαρίσοντάς τε καὶ
κωλύσοντας ἡμῶν τὴν αὔξησιν τῆς κακίας.   Pohlenz, ib. p. 620.

soul altogether. Yet it is curious to notice how true
to the Stoic presuppositions in some respects Posidonius
remained. He did not give up the belief that the soul
was itself material, a subtle invisible fire, and its abode
after death would be just as much within our stellar
system as when it was in the body. It would find itself,
on leaving the body, in the cloudy atmosphere surrounding the earth. Here, however, it would not be alone; it
would discover that the atmosphere was full of beings
like itself. The soul, the *daimōn*, who had been dwelling
in a body would be among a multitude of other *daimones*.
That was an old belief which had been endorsed by the
first disciples of Plato, and Posidonius found it reasonable. If, he argued, earth and water were inhabited by
living beings, by beings with souls, how much more
must the air, whose substance was so much more like
soul-substance, have beings in it endowed with soul and
reason! [1] And Posidonius seems to have believed that

---

[1] Εἴπερ τε ἐν γῇ καὶ θαλάσσῃ πολλῆς οὔσης παχυμερείας ποικίλα
συνίσταται ζῷα ψυχικῆς τε καὶ αἰσθητικῆς μετέχοντα δυνάμεως, πολλῷ
πιθανώτερόν ἐστιν ἐν τῷ ἀέρι, πολὺ τὸ καθαρὸν καὶ εἰλικρινὲς ἔχοντι
παρὰ τὴν γῆν καὶ τὸ ὕδωρ, ἔμψυχά τινα καὶ νοερὰ συνίστασθαι ζῷα.
καὶ τούτῳ συμφωνεῖ τὸ τοὺς Διοσκούρους ἀγαθούς τινας εἶναι δαίμονας,
σωτῆρας εὐσέλμων νεῶν, καὶ τὸ

τρὶς γὰρ μύριοί εἰσιν ἐπὶ χθονὶ πουλυβοτείρῃ
ἀθάνατοι Ζηνὸς φύλακες μερόπων ἀνθρώπων.

ἀλλ' εἰ ἐν τῷ ἀέρι πιθανὸν ὑπάρχειν ζῷα, πάντως εὔλογον καὶ ἐν τῷ
αἰθέρι ζῴων εἶναι φύσιν, ὅθεν καὶ οἱ ἄνθρωποι νοερᾶς μετέχουσι
δυνάμεως, κἀκεῖθεν αὐτὴν σπάσαντες. ὄντων δὲ αἰθερίων ζῴων, καὶ
κατὰ πολὺ τῶν ἐπιγείων ὑπερφέρειν δοκούντων τῷ ἄφθαρτα εἶναι καὶ
ἀγέννητα, δοθήσεται καὶ θεοὺς ὑπάρχειν, τούτων μὴ διαφέροντας.
Posidonius (?) *ap.* Sext. Emp. *adv. math.* ix. 86, 87.

'Mundum dividi in duas partes, caelum et terram, et caelum biforiam these *daimones* maintained an individual, imperishable existence, from one period of world-conflagration to the next. When the soul at death passed into the air it was only going back to the region whence it had come; its residence in the body was a transient episode in its life.

What happened to the disembodied *daimōn* depended, of course, upon what manner of life the individual had lived on the earth. And here Posidonius repelled some of the traditional ideas as emphatically as he endorsed others. All the accounts of penal sufferings inflicted upon the souls of the wicked, which had been a prominent part of the old Orphism and had been taken up by Plato and his disciple Xenocrates—these Posidonius the Stoic could not accept. There was no such place as the Homeric, Orphic, Platonic, Hell. Remember that he would acknowledge the existence of no world outside this material one we see, and its topography left no room for a hell anywhere. The poets seemed to place it under the ground, but that, Posidonius said, was impossible, as the earth was solid.[1]

in aethera et aëra, terram vero in aquam et humum . . . quas omnes quattuor partes animarum esse plenas. ab summo autem circuitu caeli ad circulum lunae aetherias animas esse astra ac stellas, eos caelestes deos non modo intelligi esse sed etiam videri; inter lunae vero gyrum et nimborum ac ventorum cacumina aëreas esse animas, sed eas animo non oculis videri, et vocari heroas et lares et genios.' Augustin. *De Civ. Dei*, vii. 6.

[1] 'Lucretius ex maiore parte et alii integre (*probably Posidonius among them*) docent inferorum regna nec esse quidem posse. nam locum ipsorum quem possimus dicere, cum sub terris esse dicantur Antipodes? in media vero terra eos esse nec soliditas patitur nec centrum terrae, quae si in medio mundi est, tanta eius esse profunditas non potest,

Posidonius would not even allow the view of Xenocrates, that the disembodied souls were tormented for
their sins in the air, the view which we find reflected in
some passages of the Sixth Book of the *Aeneid*.[1]   For
the *daimōn*, the divine mind in man, could only suffer
through its union with the body, and when that union
was dissolved there could be for it no more passion
and no more pain.   And yet Posidonius upheld the
distinction between the souls of the righteous and the
wicked, and nowhere, I suppose, does the Stoic materialism come in more quaintly.   For the soul, as we saw,
was literally a sort of vapour, and the effect of giving
way to passion was that the substance of the vapour got
muddy to a greater or less degree.   By a law of physics
airy and fiery substances rose in space till they reached
an environment of the same quality as themselves.   Now
the outer spheres of the world, the spheres of the fixed
stars, of the five planets and the Sun, were composed of
pure ether, but with the sphere of the Moon the divine
essence began to be mixed with baser humours, and the
air below the moon grew thicker and more turbid the
nearer you came to the centre of things, to the globe
of the earth.

The *daimōn*, therefore, who in the body had retained its
purity flew instantly on being liberated to the region of

ut medio sui habeat inferos, in quibus esse dicitur Tartarus.'   Servius *ad
Aen.* vi. 127.

[1] See Eduard Norden's introduction in his edition of the Sixth Book
of the *Aeneid*, where the affinity of Virgil with Posidonius is shown
at large.   Norden, however, does not distinguish between the view
ascribed in my lecture (following Heinze and Schmekel) to Posidonius
and the view that the purgation in the air involved penal suffering.

the pure stars, cleaving the grosser atmosphere like a
shaft of flame.[1]   But the others, more or less weighed

[1] Καὶ γὰρ οὐδὲ τὰς ψυχὰς ἔνεστιν ὑπονοῆσαι κάτω φερομένας·
λεπτομερεῖς γὰρ οὖσαι καὶ οὐχ ἧττον πυρώδεις ἢ πνευματώδεις εἰς τοὺς
ἄνω μᾶλλον τόπους κουφοφοροῦσιν. καὶ καθ' αὑτὰς δὲ διαμένουσι καὶ
οὐχ, ὡς ἔλεγεν ὁ Ἐπίκουρος, ἀπολυθεῖσαι τῶν σωμάτων καπνοῦ δίκην
σκίδνανται. οὐδὲ γὰρ πρότερον τὸ σῶμα διακρατητικὸν ἦν αὐτῶν, ἀλλ'
αὐταὶ τῷ σώματι συμμονῆς ἦσαν αἴτιαι, πολὺ δὲ πρότερον καὶ ἑαυταῖς.
ἔκσκηνοι γοῦν [ἡλίου] γενόμεναι τὸν ὑπὸ σελήνην οἰκοῦσι τόπον, ἐνθάδε
τε διὰ τὴν εἰλικρίνειαν τοῦ ἀέρος πλείονα πρὸς διαμονὴν λαμβάνουσι
χρόνον, τροφῇ τε χρῶνται οἰκείᾳ τῇ ἀπὸ γῆς ἀναθυμιάσει ὡς καὶ τὰ
λοιπὰ ἄστρα, τὸ διαλῦσόν τε αὐτὰς ἐν ἐκείνοις τοῖς τόποις οὐκ ἔχουσιν.
εἰ οὖν διαμένουσιν αἱ ψυχαί, δαίμοσιν αἱ αὐταὶ γίνονται· εἰ δὲ δαίμονές
εἰσι, ῥητέον καὶ θεοὺς ὑπάρχειν, μηδὲν αὐτῶν τὴν ὕπαρξιν βλαπτούσης
τῆς περὶ τῶν ἐν Ἅιδου μυθευομένων προλήψεως. Posidonius *apud* Sext.
Emp. *adv. math.* ix. 71–4.

'Perspicuum debet esse animos, cum e corpore excesserint, sive illi
sint animales, id est spirabiles, sive ignei, sublime ferri . . . hoc etiam
magis necesse est ferantur ad caelum et ab iis perrumpatur et dividatur
crassus hic et concretus aër, qui est terrae proximus. calidior est enim,
ve potius ardentior, animus quam est hic aër, quem modo dixi crassum
atque concretum ; quod ex eo sciri potest, quia corpora nostra terreno
principiorum genere confecta ardore animi concalescunt. accedit ut eo
facilius animus evadat ex hoc aëre, quem saepe iam appello, eumque
perrumpat, quod nihil est animo velocius : nulla est celeritas quae possit
cum animi celeritate contendere. qui si permanet incorruptus suique
similis, necesse est ita feratur, ut penetret et dividat omne caelum hoc,
in quo nubes, imbres ventique coguntur, quod et umidum et caliginosum
est propter exhalationes terrae ; quam regionem cum superavit animus
naturamque sui similem contigit et adgnovit, iunctis ex anima tenui et
ex ardore solis temperato ignibus insistit et finem altius se ecferendi
facit. tum enim sui similem et levitatem et calorem adeptus, tamque
paribus examinatus ponderibus nullam in partem movetur, eaque ei
demum naturalis est sedes, cum ad sui simile penetravit, in quo nulla
re egens aletur et sustentabitur isdem rebus, quibus astra sustentantur et
aluntur.' Cic. *Tusc. Dis.* i. 40, 42, 43.

down by the foulness they had contracted in the body,
rose only till they reached an air of their own quality.
There they remained floating till their substance regained
its clearness and they too could mount beyond the moon.
But some were so burdened with uncleanness that they
were kept close down to the earth, so close that they
were pulled back again into new bodies and once more
experienced passion and pain.   That was how they were
punished.

For the only real hell was found here on this earth,
and the impure were ever drawn back into it anew.[1]

'Qua re hoc commentemur, mihi crede, disiungamusque nos a corporibus, id est consuescamus mori.   hoc, et dum erimus in terris, erit illi
caelesti vitae simile, et cum illuc ex his vinclis emissi feremur, minus
tardabitur cursus animorum.   nam qui in compedibus corporis semper
fuerunt, etiam cum soluti sunt, tardius ingrediuntur, ut ii qui ferro vincti
multos annos fuerunt.'   Cic. *Tusc. Dis.* i. 75.

'Haec refelli possunt : sunt enim ignorantis quae de aeternitate
animorum dicantur, de mente dici, quae omni turbido motu semper
vacet, non de partibus iis, in quibus aegritudines, irae libidinesque
versentur, quas is, contra quem haec dicuntur (i. e. Plato), semotas
mente et disclusas putat.'   Cic. *Tusc. Dis.* i. 80.

[1] Στωικοὶ δὲ (i.e. Posidonius) τούτων οὐδὲν προσίενται, ἀλλ' ἐπειδὰν
ἀποχωρισθῶσι τῶν σωμάτων φασὶ τὰς ἀκρατεστέρας καὶ τῶν ἡδέων
ἐπιθυμητικὰς αὖθις [ἐφιεμένας τῶν διὰ τῶν σωμάτων ἡδονῶν προσγιγνο-
μένων] ἐγκαταδύεσθαι πάλιν τοῖς σώμασιν ἐξ ἀρχῆς καὶ μηδέποτε
παύεσθαι τούτοις περιπιπτούσας, ἕως ἂν παιδεύσεως τῆς προσηκούσης
τύχωσι καὶ τῶν καλῶν εἰς γνῶσιν ἀφικόμεναι χρηστὸν ἕλωνται βίον.
καὶ μετὰ τὴν διάλυσιν καὶ τὴν ἀπαλλαγὴν τοῦ σώματος καθ' αὐτὰς
† διαφανεῖς σπουδαίων δεομένων † (διαμένωσιν Heinze) ἰδέας μετελθούσας
(-οῦσαι Heinze), τὰς ἀγαθὰς καὶ μετὰ ταῦτα διὰ παντὸς † οὔσας τὰς
πάλιν οὕτω διακειμένας † (συνοῦσαι ταῖς πάλιν οὕτω διακειμέναις Heinze,
οὔσας ταῖς πάλαι οὕτω διακειμέναις Diels).   Galen, *Hist. Philos.* 24 =
Diels, *Dox. Graec.* p. 614, see M. Heinze, *Xenokrates,* p. 133.

'Ergo hanc terram, in qua vivimus, inferos esse voluerunt, quia est

And Heaven too was within this system of material spheres. You could see it quite plainly overhead any clear night, when you looked up into that expanse of stars, even if you could not go there. There at any rate all the souls of good men were till the next world-conflagration.

omnium circulorum infima, planetarum scilicet septem Saturni, Iovis, Martis, Solis, Veneris, Mercurii, Lunae et duorum magnorum. hinc est quod habemus : "et novies Styx interfusa coercet" (*Aen.* vi. 439), nam novem circulis cingitur terra. ergo omnia, quae de inferis finguntur, suis locis hic esse comprobabimus ; quod autem dicit ... aut poetice dictum est et secundum philosophorum altam scientiam (*Posidonius again* ?), qui deprehenderunt bene viventium animas ad superiores circulos, id est ad originem suam redire ... male viventium vero diutius in his permorari corporibus permutatione diversa et esse apud inferos semper.' Servius *ad Aen.* vi. 127.

Cf. Καὶ τῆς Στυγὸς ἐπιφερομένης αἱ ψυχαὶ βοῶσι δειμαίνουσαι· πολλὰς γὰρ ὁ Ἅιδης (i.e. the earth) ἀφαρπάζει περιολισθανούσας· ἄλλας δ' ἀνακομίζεται κάτωθεν ἡ σελήνη προσνηχομένας, αἷς εἰς καιρὸν ἡ τῆς γενέσεως τελευτὴ συνέπεσε, πλὴν ὅσαι μιαραὶ καὶ ἀκάθαρτοι· ταύτας δ' ἀστράπτουσα καὶ μυκωμένη φοβερὸν οὐκ ἐᾷ πελάζειν, ἀλλὰ θρηνοῦσαι τὸν ἑαυτῶν πότμον ἀποσφαλλόμεναι φέρονται κάτω πάλιν ἐπ' ἄλλην γένεσιν. Plutarch, *De gen. Soc.* 22 (after Posidonius, with embellishments ?).

Ἐκ δὲ δαιμόνων ὀλίγαι μὲν ἐν χρόνῳ πολλῷ δι' ἀρετῆς καθαρθεῖσαι παντάπασι θειότητος μετέσχον· ἐνίαις δὲ συμβαίνει μὴ κρατεῖν ἑαυτῶν, ἀλλ' ὑφιεμέναις καὶ ἐνδυομέναις πάλιν σώμασι θνητοῖς ἀλαμπῆ καὶ ἀμυδρὰν ζωὴν ὥσπερ ἀναθυμιάσιν ἴσχειν. Plutarch, *De def. orac.* 10.

Τούτων τῶν ψυχῶν αἱ μὲν κατίασιν ἐνδεθησόμεναι σώμασι θνητοῖς, ὅσαι προσγειόταται καὶ φιλοσώματοι, αἱ δὲ ἀνέρχονται, διακριθεῖσαι πάλιν κατὰ τοὺς ὑπὸ φύσεως ὁρισθέντας ἀριθμοὺς καὶ χρόνους. τούτων αἱ μὲν τὰ σύντροφα καὶ συνήθη τοῦ θνητοῦ βίου ποθοῦσαι παλινδρομοῦσιν αὖθις, αἱ δὲ πολλὴν φλυαρίαν αὐτοῦ καταγνοῦσαι δεσμωτήριον μὲν καὶ τύμβον ἐκάλεσαν τὸ σῶμα, φυγοῦσαι δὲ ὥσπερ ἐξ εἱρκτῆς ἢ μνήματος, ἄνω κούφοις πτεροῖς πρὸς αἰθέρα ἐξαρθεῖσαι μετεωροπολοῦσι τὸν αἰῶνα. Philo, *De somn.* i. 138 (p. 642 M.).

And Posidonius knew what they were doing. They were watching the stars go round.[1] This to us might not seem an occupation of ever-fresh interest, but the idea of it apparently suggested the perfection of bliss to the men of those days. Do you remember the striking passage in the *Georgics* where Virgil describes what he desires to gain from 'the sweet Muses, whose holy things

[1] 'Integer ille nihilque in terris relinquens sui fugit et totus excessit paulumque supra nos commoratus, dum expurgatur et inhaerentia vitia situmque omnem mortalis aevi excutit, deinde ad excelsa sublatus inter felices currit animas . . . parens tuus, Marcia, illic nepotem suum, quamquam illic omnibus omne cognatum est, adplicat sibi nova luce gaudentem et *vicinorum siderum meatus* docet, nec ex coniectura sed omnium ex vero peritus in arcana naturae libens ducit.' Seneca, *Ad Marciam de consol.* 25.

'Profecto beati erimus, cum corporibus relictis et cupiditatum et aemulationum erimus expertes; quodque nunc facimus, cum laxati curis sumus, ut spectare aliquid velimus et visere, id multo tum faciemus liberius totosque nos in contemplandis rebus perspiciendisque ponemus, propterea quod et natura inest in mentibus nostris insatiabilis quaedam cupiditas veri videndi et orae ipsae locorum illorum, quo pervenerimus, quo faciliorem nobis *cognitionem rerum caelestium*, eo maiorem cognoscendi cupiditatem dabunt . . . quod tandem spectaculum fore putamus, cum totam terram contueri licebit eiusque cum situm formam circumscriptionem tum et habitabiles regiones et rursum omni cultu propter vim frigoris aut caloris vacantes!' Cic. *Tusc. Dis.* i. 44, 45.

'Ea vita via est in caelum et in hunc coetum eorum, qui iam vixerunt et corpore laxati illum incolunt locum, quem vides . . . quem vos, ut a Graiis accepistis, orbem lacteum nuncupatis; ex quo omnia mihi contemplanti praeclara cetera et mirabilia videbantur. *erant autem eae stellae,* quas nunquam ex hoc loco vidimus, et eae magnitudines omnium, quas esse nunquam suspicati sumus, ex quibus erat ea minima, quae ultima a caelo, citima a terra luce lucebat aliena (*the moon*). stellarum autem globi terrae magnitudinem facile vincebant.' Cic. *Somn. Scip.* (*De Repub.* vi. 16).

he bears *ingenti percussus amore*'? It is, in the first place, not, as one might expect, poetical afflatus, but to understand the 'ways of the sky and the stars', to know the reason of eclipses and earthquakes and tides.[1] Those were just the desires which the disembodied souls in the upper world satisfied to their hearts' content.

And there was something else which they were conceived to do. In a passage of Plutarch, which is thought to re-echo something in Posidonius, there is described how the disembodied *daimones* do not put off all interest in the struggles of earth. They are there to encourage the souls which are hard bestead in the waves of life as they strain by self-conquest towards the haven. The soul must win its own salvation, but if after ten thousand re-births it arrives at last, spent with toil, at the shore, 'God does not grudge that its own familiar *daimōn* should give it help : nay, He allows any *daimōn* who will, to help it : and one *daimōn* is eager to help this soul to safety and another *daimōn* that, with a

---

[1] Me vero primum dulces ante omnia Musae,
   quarum sacra fero ingenti percussus amore,
   accipiant caelique vias et sidera monstrent,
   defectus solis varios lunaeque labores,
   unde tremor terris, qua vi maria alta tumescant
   obicibus ruptis, rursusque in se ipsa residant,
   quid tantum Oceano properent se tingere soles
   hiberni, vel quae tardis mora noctibus obstet.

   .   .   .   .

   felix qui potuit rerum cognoscere causas,
   atque metus omnes et inexorabile fatum
   subiecit pedibus strepitumque Acherontis avari!

   Georg. ii. 475-92.

word of cheer. And the soul hears, because the *daimōn* comes very close to it, and is saved : or if it does not hearken, the *daimōn* lets it go, and so much the worse for the soul.'[1]

You will see that when the Stoic books talked about the world as one great city, of which gods and men were citizens, it was really a much more compact and

---

[1] Ὡς γὰρ ἀθλητὰς καταλύσαντας ἄσκησιν ὑπὸ γήρως οὐ τελέως ἀπολείπει τὸ φιλότιμον καὶ φιλοσώματον, ἀλλ' ἑτέρους ἀσκοῦντας ὁρῶντες ἥδονται καὶ παρακαλοῦσι καὶ συμπαραθέουσιν· οὕτως οἱ πεπαυμένοι τῶν περὶ τὸν βίον ἀγώνων δι' ἀρετὴν ψυχῆς γενόμενοι δαίμονες οὐ παντελῶς ἀτιμάζουσι τἀνταῦθα πράγματα καὶ λόγους καὶ σπουδάς, ἀλλὰ τοῖς ἐπὶ ταὐτὸ γυμναζομένοις τέλος εὐμενεῖς ὄντες καὶ συμφιλοτιμούμενοι πρὸς τὴν ἀρετήν, ἐγκελεύονται καὶ συνεξορμῶσιν, ὅταν ἐγγὺς ἤδη τῆς ἐλπίδος ἁμιλλωμένους καὶ ψαύοντας ὁρῶσιν. οὐ γὰρ οἷς ἔτυχε συμφέρεται τὸ δαιμόνιον· ἀλλ' οἷον ἐπὶ τῶν νηχομένων ἐν θαλάττῃ τοὺς μὲν πελαγίους ἔτι καὶ πρόσω τῆς γῆς φερομένους οἱ ἐπὶ γῆς ἑστῶτες σιωπῇ θεῶνται μόνον, τοὺς δ' ἐγγὺς ἤδη παραθέοντες καὶ παρεμβαίνοντες ἅμα καὶ χειρὶ καὶ φωνῇ βοηθοῦντες ἀνασώζουσιν· οὕτως, ὦ ⟨Σιμμία⟩, τοῦ δαιμονίου ὁ τρόπος. ⟨ἐᾷ γὰρ ἡμᾶς⟩ βαπτιζομένους ὑπὸ τῶν πραγμάτων, καὶ σώματα πολλὰ καθάπερ ὀχήματα μεταλαμβάνοντας, αὐτοὺς ἐξαμιλλᾶσθαι καὶ μακροθυμεῖν, δι' οἰκείας πειρωμένους ἀρετῆς σώζεσθαι καὶ τυγχάνειν λιμένος. ἥτις δ' ἂν ἤδη διὰ μυρίων γενέσεων ἠγωνισμένη μακροὺς ἀγῶνας εὖ καὶ προθύμως ψυχή, τῆς περιόδου συμπεραινομένης κινδυνεύουσα καὶ φιλοτιμουμένη περὶ τὴν ἔκβασιν ἱδρῶτι πολλῷ ἄνω προσφέρηται, ταύτῃ τὸν οἰκεῖον οὐ νεμεσᾷ δαίμονα βοηθεῖν ὁ θεὸς ἀλλ' ἀφίησι τῷ προθυμουμένῳ· προθυμεῖται δ' ἄλλος ἄλλην ἀνασῴζειν ἐγκελευόμενος· ἡ δὲ συνακούει διὰ τὸ πλησιάζειν καὶ σῴζεται· μὴ πειθομένη δέ, ἀπολιπόντος τοῦ δαίμονος, οὐκ εὐτυχῶς ἀπαλλάσσει. Plutarch, *De gen. Soc.* 24.

Cf. the office of the Angels (οἱ τοῦ θεοῦ λόγοι) in Philo : Συγκαταβαίνοντες διὰ φιλανθρωπίαν καὶ ἔλεον τοῦ γένους ἡμῶν, ἐπικουρίας ἕνεκα καὶ συμμαχίας, ἵνα καὶ τὴν ἔτι ὥσπερ ἐν ποταμῷ, τῷ σώματι, φορουμένην ψυχὴν σωτήριον πνέοντες ἀναζωῶσι. *De Somn.* i. 147.

knowable whole which was presented to their imaginations than is suggested by the Universe to ours.
Even to Posidonius, indeed, the spaces of the heavens
were vast, as compared with the globe of Earth, yet
he could see the fiery orbs which marked the outer
boundary of the universe, the *flammantia moenia mundi*,
and there was nothing beyond. There were no possibilities of modes of being and life altogether outside
the field of the senses, to make Posidonius uneasy.
The whole of Reality was for him contained within
the envelope of fiery ether, one world, knit together by
a natural sympathy between all the parts.

This sympathy between the parts was a leading idea
of Stoicism, to which Posidonius apparently gave fresh
emphasis. It was the basis for the Stoic theory of
Divination. An abstract from his work on divination
may probably be discerned in the First Book of Cicero's
De Divinatione. According to this, Posidonius distinguished two sorts of divination, the scientific (*artificiosa*)
and the natural. *Scientific* divination consisted in the
methodical observing, over sufficiently long periods of
time, of the connexion which particular signs had with
particular events. The connexion might be established
empirically even if one could not give the explanation
of it. The explanation, indeed, might be just that
God had ordered the whole process of things from the
beginning as a coherent design, and Time was but the
uncoiling of a rope which existed already complete in
the Divine Purpose. *Natural* divination, on the other
hand, did not rest on any logical inference. It was an
immediate communication from God or disembodied

daimones to the soul, when its bodily faculties were neutralized in sleep or frenzy—or it might be that the embodied *daimōn* in us had an immense fund of experience gathered through countless ages in converse with innumerable other souls, a fund of experience accessible to us only when the tumult and stir of the bodily senses was stilled.[1]   Especially for one sort of divination which was coming to dominate the Greco-Roman world did the doctrine of the sympathy of the universe purport to give a rational basis—for the new science of Astrology.[2]   A great deal of the thrill with which men looked up to the stars, which made them think, as we saw, that the contemplation of their move-

---

[1] 'Tribus modis censet (Posidonius) deorum adpulsu homines somniare, uno, quod provideat animus ipse per sese, quippe qui deorum cognatione teneatur, altero quod plenus aër sit immortalium animorum, in quibus tanquam insignitae notae veritatis appareant, tertio, quod ipsi di cum dormientibus conloquantur.'   Cic. *De Div.* i. 64.

'Altera divinatio est naturalis, ut ante dixi ; quae physica disputandi subtilitate referenda est ad naturam deorum, a qua, ut doctissimis sapientissimisque placuit, haustos animos et libatos habemus ; cumque omnia completa et referta sint aeterno sensu et mente divina, necesse est cognatione divinorum animorum animos humanos commoveri.   Sed vigilantes animi vitae necessitatibus serviunt diiunguntque se a societate divina vinclis corporis impediti.'   ib. 110.

'Viget enim animus in somnis liber ab sensibus omnique impeditione curarum iacente et mortuo paene corpore.   qui quia vixit ab omni aeternitate versatusque est cum innumerabilibus animis, omnia quae in natura rerum sunt, videt, si modo temperatis escis modicisque potionibus ita est adfectus, ut sopito corpore ipse vigilet.   haec somniantis est divinatio.'   ib. 115.

[2] 'Astrology fell upon the Hellenistic mind as a new disease falls upon some remote island people' (Gilbert Murray, *Four Stages of Greek Religion*, p. 125).

ments was the chief part of the bliss of heaven, came from the belief that those movements were connected by some occult natural necessity with the events on earth. There is evidence that Posidonius, whose interest covered the whole field of science, did not neglect Astrology. But there is the less need to enter upon this topic, as it has been treated by Cumont in his lectures published last year under the title *Astrology and Religion among the Greeks and Romans*. Here, too, Posidonius is a conspicuous figure. Cumont is so great an authority on these subjects that if any of his statements appear to one questionable, one must suspect that this is due to one's own imperfect knowledge. I should, however, like to suggest for re-consideration his view that Posidonius adulterated Stoicism with the religious traditions of the Syrians. That Posidonius came from Syria is true ; but, as we saw, he appears to have left his home early and to have regarded his fellow countrymen with contempt. So far as I can see, Posidonius cannot be proved to have incorporated with Stoicism anything more than was already found in the Platonic-Pythagorean tradition.

Even so, however, there would be a sense in which it was true that Posidonius, as Cumont says, was an agent in bringing about a syncretism between East and West. If his philosophy was itself restricted to traditions which had already good Hellenic sanction, it did, no doubt, exhibit those traditions in a form, into which it was peculiarly easy to fit Oriental accessories later on. There is an undeniable family resemblance between his world, in which the souls rise through grosser air to the spheres of divine ether, and the worlds of the Gnostics a century or two later, where the souls strive to make their way upward through the demon-guarded spheres of the Seven Planets to the sphere of light and bliss beyond. Again, the doctrine of Posidonius that in the childhood of the human race men had lived in holy innocence, nearer in spirit to the divine ;[1] his doctrine that the soul might receive direct enlightenment from beings not in the body, apart from all processes of the reason—all that, of course, blended easily with those beliefs in a tradition going back to some primitive revelation, or to some more recent prophet, which were characteristic of Eastern religions and Gnostic sects. We can understand that many a Greek later on, whose thought had been shaped by Posidonius, had categories ready, when he encountered the new conceptions which were penetrating the Hellenistic world from the East; that many a Jew, like Philo, when he wished to present his faith to the Greek world in terms of Greek philosophy, found much in Posidonius that only wanted a little manipulation to carry his message.

It was not the triumph of Christianity which was fatal to the world-view, one variety of which is represented by Posidonius; perhaps, indeed, that view never had more splendid expression than in the great Christian poem which came from the heart of mediaeval Italy. What was fatal to it was the triumph of Copernicus. Man, if he limited his view to the material world, was once more a mote in an unfathomable universe.

[1] Seneca, *Epist.* 90. 5 f. 'non negaverim fuisse alti spiritus viros et, ut ita dicam, *a dis recentes* ' (§ 44).

Le silence éternel de ces espaces infinis m'effraie; it was a few generations after Copernicus that Pascal wrote that. For centuries man had held in his hands a certain chart of the world which gave him assurance and comfort. And now that chart was discovered to be no good.

LECTURE IV

THE SCEPTICS

LECTURE IV
THE SCEPTICS

As soon as the human spirit awoke to see in the old familiar world an enigma, a problem, an unexplored mystery, there were many confident enough to undertake its discovery, ready to hold a belief as to what lay beyond the field of the senses—to believe and affirm. It was this buoyant hope which nerved Greek philosophy when it first came into being with Thales and the Ionians, which nerved it all through its long spiritual travail up to Plato and Aristotle, to Zeno and Epicurus. And yet in the very effort there came ever and again the revulsion of despair, the sick feeling that the effort was no good, that there was no winning any real knowledge from the void. That disconsolate sceptical note is heard even in the young adventurous days of Greek philosophy—in Xenophanes :

'The certain truth there is no man who knows, nor ever shall be, about the Gods and all the things whereof I speak. Yea, even if a man should chance to say something utterly right, still he himself knows it not: there is nothing anywhere but guessing' [1]—

---

[1] Καὶ τὸ μὲν οὖν σαφὲς οὔτις ἀνὴρ γένετ' οὐδέ τις ἔσται
εἰδὼς ἀμφὶ θεῶν τε καὶ ἄσσα λέγω περὶ πάντων·
εἰ γὰρ καὶ τὰ μάλιστα τύχοι τετελεσμένον εἰπών,
αὐτὸς ὅμως οὐκ οἶδε· δόκος δ' ἐπὶ πᾶσι τέτυκται.

Frag. 34, Diels.

or in Empedocles :

‘ When they have but looked upon the little portion of their own life, they fly away in a moment, like smoke, persuaded each one of that particular thing only with which he has come into contact as they are driven hither and thither, and yet each one flatters himself that he has found the whole; so far are these things beyond the reach of men, not to be seen of the eye, or heard of the ear, or comprehended with the mind.’ [1]

The very affirmations which philosophers made, from Thales onwards, produced in many minds a reaction of doubt, for affirmation was soon clashing with affirmation, and the theory which was promulgated one day as the latest truth was before long superseded by another. In the philosophers whom we have quoted, the sceptical doubt haunted only the background of their consciousness and did not find utterance except in momentary phases of thought. But there must have been many people whom the disputes of philosophers discouraged from putting any faith in philosophy at all. Such people may have been much more numerous than the fragments of old Greek philosophical writing show. For scepticism is naturally less vocal than dogmatism. We know something of the men who had a theory to propagate, and contended for it with voice or pen, but we know nothing of all those who shrugged

---

[1] Παῦρον δὲ ζωῆς ἰδίου μέρος ἀθρήσαντες
ὠκύμοροι καπνοῖο δίκην ἀρθέντες ἀπέπταν
αὐτὸ μόνον πεισθέντες, ὅτῳ προσέκυρσεν ἕκαστος
πάντοσ᾽ ἐλαυνόμενοι, τὸ δ᾽ ὅλον ⟨πᾶς⟩ εὔχεται εὑρεῖν.
οὕτως οὔτ᾽ ἐπιδερκτὰ τάδ᾽ ἀνδράσι οὐδ᾽ ἐπακουστὰ
οὔτε νόῳ περιληπτά.   Frag. 2, Diels.

their shoulders and went their way. It is only where
scepticism itself becomes a formulated theory that it
leaves record of itself in the history of philosophy.

The man who is reckoned the Founder of Scepticism
as a definite tradition was a contemporary of the men
who founded the two great dogmatic systems of Stoicism
and Epicureanism. Pyrrho of Elis was there to mark
all dogma with a query. We cannot be exactly sure
what he taught, since he left no writing and stands
rather as a strong problematic figure at the back of the
Sceptical tradition, just as Socrates stands behind the
Platonic. We know for one thing that he went with
Alexander the Great to India. Wild statements have
often been made as to Indian influences travelling
Westward. In this case there is good ground for
believing that upon a day more than two thousand years
ago, under the sky of the Punjab, this Greek, his mind
full of Homer and Democritus, did come face to face
with dark impassive *sannyasis*, their minds full of another
world of things. It is a moment which kindles the historical imagination. Unfortunately just here, where the
contact is provable, no transmission of Indian doctrine
can be traced. It was only the memory of that strange
impassiveness and detachment which Pyrrho seems to
have carried away; it was that which he strove in his
after life to reproduce. Probably the Indian sages had
no particular desire to instruct the alien from the West,
and ignorance of each other's language would in any
case have limited the communication of metaphysical
ideas.

What Pyrrho taught we can only know from the

accounts of others, notably of his disciple, Timon of Phlius. Apparently the two main influences in his scepticism were, on the one hand, Democritus, who had laid stress on the merely subjective character of sensation—*νόμῳ γλυκὺ καὶ νόμῳ πικρόν*—and on the other hand the Sophistic criticism. Democritus had had his own dogma—*ἐτεῇ δὲ ἄτομα καὶ κενόν*—and here Pyrrho would not follow. He took up the old contention of Protagoras. Every affirmation could be logically confronted with its opposite : the clash of dogmas was not something to be surprised at : the conflict belonged to the very nature of dogma. This was the principle of *isostheneia*, equal strength on both sides of every question, which became a stock part of Greek Scepticism. It really, I suppose, was doing no more than giving a stereotyped label and formulation to what had been the inarticulate feeling all along of those whom the endless controversies of the schools had repelled. Many a plain man, as I suggested, had probably determined in consequence not to bother himself with philosophy, and this was just what Pyrrho's wisdom came to, *ataraxia*, not to bother oneself. The unhappy desire to know was the cause of all the fever and fret, the polemical passion and torturing doubt. Once grasp that the desire was essentially futile, that you could let the mind play and *hold it back* all the while from fixed belief (*epochē*), and there was no reason why you should not be perfectly happy and contented in nescience. It was a wonderful deliverance to realize that you need not mind not knowing. This, apparently, was Pyrrho's gospel. It was not inspired by an acute intellect analysing the process of thought and coming to a sceptical conclusion; it was strikingly different from the modern Agnosticism which often goes with a vigorous interest in 'Science'; it was the expression of weariness, of disgust with the endless strife of tongues, of the relief found in mere ceasing from effort and stagnation. In the fragments of the satirical poems of Timon, which are our first-hand evidence for this early phase of Scepticism, the hatred of wind-bags, of empty talk, of the pretentious assumption of knowledge, is the one motive running through all. It is really so simple— not to bother and to have done with all the fuss.

This, I suggested, was strikingly different from modern Agnosticism. In its spirit and practical working it does seem to me utterly unlike; but one must allow that if one looks at its theoretical first principles, there is rather striking resemblance. The principle familiar to us in modern Agnosticism, that you can know phenomena and their sequences but you cannot know the Reality which lies behind them, was already enunciated almost in the same words by ancient Scepticism. 'We do not use our sceptical phrases', says Sextus Empiricus, 'about everything in the world without distinction. We use them only of things inaccessible to the senses and investigated by the way of dogma. The phenomenon we affirm as an appearance to ourselves; we do not make positive statements about the nature of the external objects in themselves.'[1] 'Man (as distinguished from other

<hr>

[1] Οὐ περὶ πάντων τῶν πραγμάτων καθόλου φαμὲν αὐτάς, ἀλλὰ περὶ

animals) has in the sphere of phenomena (ἐν τοῖς φαινομένοις) a faculty of following the process of things and retaining it (τηρητικήν τινα ἔχειν ἀκολουθίαν). In virtue of this he remembers what phenomena he has observed accompanying each other, what preceding and what coming after, so that when the first members of the sequence are presented to him the rest are revived.'[1] Thus, as is explained in another passage, the Sceptic did not refrain from inferring fire when he saw smoke, or a wound when he saw a scar.[2] These passages are taken from a writer of the second century A.D., Sextus Empiricus, but the principles enunciated seem to go back to Timon, the immediate disciple of Pyrrho. A sentence is preserved from his work Περὶ αἰσθήσεων : 'That honey is sweet I refuse to assert ; that it appears sweet, I fully grant.' In another work the line occurred 'The phenomenon is always valid'. And he maintained that he had not gone against

τῶν ἀδήλων καὶ τῶν δογματικῶς ζητουμένων, καὶ . . . τὸ φαινόμενον ἡμῶν φαμὲν καὶ οὐχὶ διαβεβαιωτικῶς περὶ τῆς φύσεως τῶν ἐκτὸς ὑποκειμένων ἀποφαινόμεθα. Sext. Emp. *Hyp.* i. 208.

[1] Κἂν δῶμεν δὲ διαφέρειν τῶν ἄλλων ζῴων τὸν ἄνθρωπον λόγῳ τε καὶ μεταβατικῇ φαντασίᾳ καὶ ἐν τῇ ἀκολουθίᾳ, ἀλλ' οὔ τοί γε καὶ ἐν τοῖς ἀδήλοις καὶ ἀνεπικρίτως διαπεφωνημένοις συγχωρήσομεν αὐτὸν εἶναι τοιοῦτον, ἐν δὲ τοῖς φαινομένοις τηρητικήν τινα ἔχειν ἀκολουθίαν, καθ' ἣν μνημονεύων τίνα μετὰ τίνων τεθεώρηται καὶ τίνα πρὸ τίνων καὶ τίνα μετὰ τίνα, ἐκ τῆς τῶν προτέρων ὑποπτώσεως ἀνανεοῦται τὰ λοιπά. Sext. Emp. *adv. math.* viii. 288.

[2] Τὸ γὰρ ὑπομνηστικὸν πεπίστευται ὑπὸ τοῦ βίου, ἐπεὶ καπνὸν ἰδών τις σημειοῦται πῦρ καὶ οὐλὴν θεασάμενος τραῦμα γεγενῆσθαι λέγει. ὅθεν οὐ μόνον οὐ μαχόμεθα τῷ βίῳ ἀλλὰ καὶ συναγωνιζόμεθα. Sext. Emp. *Hyp.* ii. 102.

the common practice of humanity.[1]   Now such principles, one would think, have only to be extended in their application in order to give us all that is required by modern scientific Agnosticism. The ancient Sceptic, however, never contemplated such extension. You could only, according to him, infer something you did not see from something you did see, when you had actually observed those things, or precisely similar things, in connexion. A theory, for instance, like the atomic theory, or, to take a favourite instance of Sextus, the theory of pores in the body, was repudiated, because atoms and pores were things which could never come within the range of sense-perception. That is to say, the immense part which working hypothesis has played in modern science was far from his thought.

There seems to us so obvious a line dividing scientific hypotheses which are based upon precise observation and experiment, accurate measurement and mathematical formulae, from metaphysical and ethical theories, into which numerical measurement cannot enter, that we find it hard, perhaps, to realize that from the standpoint of the ancient Sceptic the difference between physical and metaphysical hypotheses was much less plain. There were plenty of physical hypotheses current in the fourth century B.C.—some,

---

[1] Ὅθεν καὶ ὁ Τίμων ἐν τῷ Πύθωνί φησι μὴ ἐκβεβηκέναι τὴν συνήθειαν. καὶ ἐν τοῖς Ἰνδαλμοῖς οὕτω λέγει,

ἀλλὰ τὸ φαινόμενον πάντη σθένει οὗπερ ἂν ἔλθῃ,

καὶ ἐν τοῖς Περὶ αἰσθήσεων φησί· Τὸ μέλι ὅτι ἐστὶ γλυκὺ οὐ τίθημι, τὸ δ' ὅτι φαίνεται ὁμολογῶ. Diog. Laert. ix. 105.

like the atomic theory, anticipations of recent scientific theories—but in default of all instruments for minute observation and measurement, they were all shots in the dark.[1] What science could there be in the modern sense without the microscope, without the thermometer, without even the watch ? The modern scientist must find it hard to transport himself in imagination into such a state of things.

What seems to be the better tradition as to the Sceptical school asserts that Timon of Phlius left no disciple.[2] The school, as a school, ceased. But its soul, one might say, migrated elsewhere and reappeared in the Academy, which thereby entered another phase of its history. Timon seems for the last forty years of his long life (from about 275 to 235 B.C.) to have made Athens his home. The man who for the greater part of this time sat in the seat of Plato was Arcesilaus, a native of Pitane in Asia Minor. He, too, is among the philosophers who left no writings, and whom it is therefore hard for us now to estimate at their real value. We only know of Arcesilaus that his personality was one which shone conspicuously in the eyes of contemporaries. 'By a singular conjunction at this moment,' wrote Eratosthenes with enthusiasm, 'one city wall contained two philosophers of such eminence as Aristo and Arcesilaus'[3]—hardly two

---

[1] Σφόδρα χαριέντως ἀπεικάζουσιν οἱ σκεπτικοὶ τοὺς περὶ ἀδήλων ζητοῦντας τοῖς ἐν σκότῳ ἐπί τινα σκοπὸν τοξεύουσιν. Sext. Emp. adv. math. viii. 325.

[2] Diog. Laert. ix. 115.

[3] Ἐγένοντο γάρ, φησίν, ὡς οὐδέποτε, κατὰ τοῦτον τὸν καιρὸν ὑφ' ἕνα

names which occur to us now as luminaries of this
magnitude among all the great names of Athens.   The
notices make us think of Arcesilaus as a man of
aristocratic temper, with a certain elegant splendour in
his way of living, for he had wealth and knew how to
use it, at once fastidious and generous.   He was, we
gather, one of those minds for whom the intellectual
play of 'for' and 'against' had its fascination, apart
from the desire to arrive at a stable conclusion.
Argument was the breath of his nostrils.   Under the
new system which he introduced into the Academy,
instead of an authoritative lecture *ex cathedra*, a thesis
was set up by one of the students, whom Arcesilaus proceeded to cross-examine in Socratic fashion,
or he himself argued first on one and then on the
other side of a question.   For such a mind the
doctrine of Pyrrho, which Timon was here in Athens
to expound, had natural attraction.   It would appeal
to him, not as a relief from endless dispute, but
as keeping the possibility of argument endlessly open.
It could never come to rest in a dogmatic conclusion.
Arcesilaus took over the Pyrrhonic Scepticism so fully
that it became a question what monopoly he left to
the school which had originally enunciated it.   Timon
seems to have been at pains, so long as Arcesilaus
lived, to show that the new Scepticism of the Academy
was not of the genuine brand : the Academy was still
in bondage.   'What are you doing here, where we

περίβολον καὶ μίαν πόλιν οἱ κατ᾽ ᾽Αρίστωνα καὶ ᾽Αρκεσίλαον ἀνθήσαντες
φιλόσοφοι.   Strabo, i. 2, 2, C. 15.

free men are?' he is said to have called out to
Arcesilaus once, when he saw him passing.[1] And
Sextus Empiricus tries to show how the shreds
of dogmatism still adhered to Arcesilaus and the
Academics. What he alleges, however, to prove it
does not seem borne out by what we can ascertain of
their real doctrine. Arcesilaus, so Sextus says, affirmed
as an objective truth that the holding back of assent
was a good, whereas the true Sceptic only stated that
it *seemed* such to him.[2] If this had been the case,
Arcesilaus would, of course, have been convicted of
the shreds of dogmatism ; but according to other
accounts the Scepticism of Arcesilaus did not stop
short of declaring freely that the unknowableness of
Reality was itself doubtful.[3] This, of course, purported
to meet the obvious objection which the opponents of
Scepticism always brought up against it : 'At any rate
you assert your own fundamental principle, that the
Truth behind phenomena is unknowable.' And the
stock answer given by the later Sceptics seems to have
been that even their fundamental principle was put
forth with a query : the Sceptical philosophy was like
a drug which removed itself as well as other substances

[1] Τί σὺ δεῦρο, ἔνθαπερ ἡμεῖς οἱ ἐλεύθεροι; Diog. Laert. ix. 114.

[2] Ὁ μέντοι Ἀρκεσίλαος . . . πάνυ μοι δοκεῖ τοῖς Πυρρωνείοις
κοινωνεῖν λόγοις, ὡς μίαν εἶναι σχεδὸν τὴν κατ' αὐτὸν ἀγωγὴν καὶ τὴν
ἡμετέραν . . . πλὴν εἰ μὴ λέγοι τις ὅτι ἡμεῖς μὲν κατὰ τὸ φαινόμενον
ἡμῖν ταῦτα λέγομεν καὶ οὐ διαβεβαιωτικῶς, ἐκεῖνος δὲ ὡς πρὸς τὴν
φύσιν, ὥστε καὶ ἀγαθὸν μὲν εἶναι αὐτὴν λέγειν τὴν ἐποχήν, κακὸν δὲ
τὴν συγκατάθεσιν. Sext. Emp. *Hyp.* i. 232, 233.

[3] 'Itaque Arcesilas negabat esse quidquam quod sciri posset, ne illud
quidem ipsum, quod Socrates sibi reliquisset.' Cic. *Ac. Post.* i. § 45.

from the body.[1]   The philosopher hard-pressed not
seldom finds refuge in a figure.

The distinctive note in the Scepticism of Arcesilaus,
so far as we can trace it, was given by its special
direction against the new dogmatic system being constructed in Athens, which we considered in our first
two lectures.   If on the one side a great practical need
impelled the teachers of the new dogma, on the other
side there was something in the Hellenic spirit which
could not but rise up in opposition.   And the Stoic
epistemology, framed under the exigency of finding
some absolutely certain basis for dogma, did, as we saw,
offer only too easy a mark for philosophic criticism.
It was a weak part in the defences which naturally drew
down the attack of a man like Arcesilaus.   The Stoic
certainty was built upon the *kataleptike phantasia*, the
impression which left no room for error, because the
reality behind it could only be one thing.   It all stood
upon the assumption that there *were* impressions which
left no possible alternative.   And this is just what
Arcesilaus denied.   And if there were no such impressions, the Stoic sage who gave his absolute belief with
entire inerrancy was a figment.   On the other hand,
the Wise Man, Arcesilaus said, never believed heavily in
that way; he never, as it were, let his centre of gravity

---

[1] Περὶ πασῶν γὰρ τῶν σκεπτικῶν φωνῶν ἐκεῖνο χρὴ προειληφέναι
ὅτι περὶ τοῦ ἀληθεῖς αὐτὰς εἶναι πάντως οὐ διαβεβαιούμεθα, ὅπου γε
καὶ ὑφ' ἑαυτῶν αὐτὰς ἀναιρεῖσθαι λέγομεν δύνασθαι, συμπεριγραφομένας
ἐκείνοις περὶ ὧν λέγονται, καθάπερ τὰ καθαρτικὰ τῶν φαρμάκων οὐ
μόνον τοὺς χυμοὺς ὑπεξαιρεῖ τοῦ σώματος ἀλλὰ καὶ ἑαυτὰ τοῖς χυμοῖς
συνεξάγει. Sext. Emp. *Hyp.* i. 206.

go over upon any conviction; he saved himself from error by always withholding his assent.

About eighty years after the death of Arcesilaus, the seat of Plato passed to one whose personality stamped itself upon the later philosophical tradition — the Cyrenaean Carneades. Unfortunately, like Arcesilaus, Carneades left practically no writing behind him, so that all we know of his teaching comes through his disciple Clitomachus. Let us look at the disciple before we turn to the master. Clitomachus is interesting as a figure, because he was an example of the spread of Hellenism in that age among people not of Greek blood. He was a Semite from Carthage, and his original name was Hasdrubal. Besides his Greek works, he seems to have written books in Punic, rendering no doubt the conceptions of Greek philosophy in a tongue akin to Hebrew—books which would, one may suppose, be of singular interest to-day to Rabbinical scholars. The time came when this alien sat as master in Plato's Academy, for the Greeks apparently had no prejudice against men of non-Hellenic blood who were qualified by education to enter their society. If Carneades did not write at all, his disciple Hasdrubal-Clitomachus made up for it by the vast volume of his writing—more than 400 books, we are told. Through them the voice of Carneades reached subsequent generations.

Carneades was like his predecessor Arcesilaus in his passion for argument, his way of exhibiting the strength of both the opposing sides on each question, but one gathers that in contrast with the urbanity and aristocratic manner of Arcesilaus, there was something uncouth and violent about him. We hear of his uncut hair and neglected nails, and how the director of the gymnasium neighbouring the place where he taught had to send him a message begging him not to shout so. There was a destructive eagerness about him, which made him take a wicked delight in tearing to pieces all the dogmatic systems established in the schools. His cleverness and command of words made him terribly effective, and people went to his lectures to learn rhetoric no less than to learn philosophy. One cannot wonder that when a man of this kind electrified Rome in 156 B.C. by a brilliant oration on the thesis that righteousness was based entirely on convenience, stalwart old conservatives like Cato the Censor saw in Greek philosophy a danger to the State.

So far as one can make out, the principles of Carneades did not differ essentially from those which the Academy had already derived from Arcesilaus. The importance of Carneades is probably rather to be found in the rhetorical cleverness which gave much wider currency and popularity to the Sceptical arguments throughout the Greek world, and in his furnishing the opponents of established beliefs in Providence, in Divination, in Fate with an armoury of stock arguments, such as we meet with in Cicero and the later Sceptics. If Carneades made any original contribution to philosophy, it was apparently in his elaborating a theory of belief based on degrees of probability. The putting forward of probability (τὸ πιθανόν) as a substitute for the certain knowledge claimed by the dogmatists was what people specially connected with the name of Carneades. His theory seems to have taken its start here too from the doctrine of Arcesilaus. We shall see in a moment, when we come to the Sceptic rule of living, that Arcesilaus had found a guiding principle in the idea of the 'reasonable' (τὸ εὔλογον). The 'probable' of Carneades was, modern books tell us, the 'reasonable' of Arcesilaus, only transferred from the sphere of conduct to the sphere of knowledge. The transference was perhaps not as important in its working out, as it might appear. The 'probable' has indeed reference to the question 'What is true?' whereas the 'reasonable' has reference to the question 'What is good to do?'—in so far Carneades may naturally seem to turn his interest from practice to knowledge. But when we look at the actual context of appeals to the probable, we find that the intellectual illumination is always represented, not as the satisfaction of a speculative curiosity about the world, but as affording light for practice.[1] Perhaps Carneades felt more vividly than Arcesilaus that conduct could be reasonable only if it were guided by a judgement of some kind—knowledge or conjecture—as to what things *are*. Hence, Scepticism having destroyed the basis of certain belief, Carneades felt the need of his system of probability. The older Sceptics had said, 'The Wise Man will always withhold his assent and, knowledge being unattainable, will keep his mind immune from opinion.' Carneades seems to have found this not quite satisfactory. It was plain, of course, that if you allowed the Wise Man to hold an

[1] Goedeckemeyer, p. 65, note 2.

opinion you exposed him to error. Well, you must take the risk of that, Carneades said : it is no good trying to get the Wise Man out of the necessity of giving any sort of assent, because to act on an hypothesis is to assent to it practically, and the Wise Man, we are all agreed, must act sometimes. Hence Carneades boldly maintained in opposition to his predecessors that the Wise Man *would* hold opinions (δοξάσειν τὸν σοφόν) ; only his opinions would be limited to the sphere of things which determined conduct, i.e. phenomena—not the background of phenomena, gods and so on—and would be regulated according to degrees of probability.

The ferment which the restless criticism of Carneades and Clitomachus spread through the schools no doubt worked more or less for centuries. But their successors in the Academy, Philo of Larissa and still more Antiochus of Ascalon, found the Sceptical position an uncomfortable one in the long run to maintain, and with Antiochus the Academy practically surrendered to the Stoa. The Sceptical spirit had to find a new incarnation, and found it in a man who professed to go back behind the Academy to the purer Scepticism of Pyrrho and Timon. This was a man from the old Cretan city of Cnossos, who lived and wrote in Alexandria, Aenesidemus. It seems to be made out that he was a contemporary of Cicero's, probably a younger contemporary, whom Cicero either never heard of or did not think a person of enough account to mention. With Aenesidemus, however, Scepticism entered upon a new period of life which extended over the first two centuries of the Roman Empire, especially, it would seem, in connexion

with the 'Empiric' school of medicine.   It is this con-
cluding phase of ancient Scepticism which has delivered
to us the one systematic first-hand exposition of it which
we possess, the treatises of Sextus Empiricus, dating
from the second half of the second century A.D.

There does not seem any ground for regarding either
Aenesidemus or any of his followers as thinkers who
contributed any really new thoughts to the Sceptical
tradition.   The substance of Sextus Empiricus probably
goes back to Timon, four or five hundred years before.
The fundamental principle that the *phainomenon* alone,
each man's sensations and inferences as a fact of consciousness, was certain—this was all through the same.
The great argument against dogmatic assurance, the
disagreement of one individual with another, the disagreement of the same individual with himself under
varying circumstances, this too was the same.   In
whatever field of things disagreement was possible, in
that field there could be no dogmatic assurance, because
the question could always be raised whether what
determined my belief in opposition to some other man's
was not the personal equation in some form, behind
which I obviously could not get, however much I might
try, because it was involved in my very efforts to think
it away.   The only field of certain knowledge therefore
left was the field where agreement was universal, τὸ
κοινῶς πᾶσι φαινόμενον,[1] 'common sense', in the
literal meaning of the phrase—the field of sensation.
The sensation of white, for instance, or the sensation of
sweetness is the same for everybody, although the

[1] Sext. Emp. *adv. math.* viii. 8.

colour and taste of a particular thing might differ according to the individual percipient.[1] And all that we could do, if we did not mean to step into the dark region of things Unknowable, τὰ ἄδηλα, was just to remember what sensations we had found coupled in experience and, when we met with one, to expect the other.

What Aenesidemus did was not to produce a new variety of Scepticism, but, at a time when every one was turning to some form of dogmatism, he gathered up the Sceptical criticism which the schools, he saw, had dodged without meeting, and launched it again upon the world in a more systematic, more closely reasoned, more compact and manageable form, a stereotyped series of arguments. This was the significance of the ten 'Modes' (τρόποι) connected with his name—a presentation in detail of the kinds of disagreement intended by Sceptics when they made disagreement a ground for the withholding of assent. The first Mode is the disagreement in perception and physical qualities between men and other animals, the second is disagreement between different sorts of men, the third between the different senses in the same individual, and so on, ending up with disagreements in the sphere of conduct, customs, and laws, of mythological and philosophic belief. Similarly, Aenesidemus drew up a list of eight fallacies committed by dogmatic philosophers in professing to give an

---

[1] Ὅτι γὰρ τὰ φαινόμενα ἐπ᾽ ἴσης φαίνεται τοῖς ἀπαραποδίστους ἔχουσι τὰς αἰσθήσεις συμφανές· οὐ γὰρ ἄλλοις ἄλλως τὸ λευκὸν φαίνεται, οὐδὲ ἄλλοις ἄλλως τὸ μέλαν, οὐδὲ διαφερόντως τὸ γλυκύ, ἀλλ᾽ ὁμοίως πάντας κινεῖ. Sext. Emp. adv. math. viii. 240.

account of the causes behind phenomena. Of course, all this tabulation of the Sceptical arguments under fixed heads was a great furtherance to their popular circulation, even if it added nothing to their substance. You can find them in Sextus Empiricus and in the summary of Sceptical teaching given by Laertius Diogenes.

One cannot say that the writings of Sextus Empiricus, although they contain many interesting things, are great literature, and often there are pages together of nothing but quibbling and logic-chopping, a mere juggling with counters. But the Sceptical School in the second century A.D. had also among its adherents the most brilliant literary man of the twilight of Hellenism, Lucian of Samosata. Anybody who wants to read the case for Scepticism in a more agreeable form than the treatises of Sextus had better turn to the dialogue of Lucian which bears the name of *Hermotimus*. Many people have read an abridged and somewhat altered version of it in *Marius the Epicurean*. It seems to me a little work not unworthy to be set with Plato's. Here, too, we have the playful irony and the dramatic touches, and behind it all the pathos, the inner tragedy, which lie at the heart of scepticism. The edge of that light mockery bites as shrewdly, its arrows are as penetrating to-day, it seems to me, as eighteen centuries ago. Pater has made Hermotimus into a young man; this misses a point in the original where he is a man well on in life, who for twenty years has been labouring to find Truth along the Stoic path and not attained; he hopes that he may attain, perhaps in twenty years more. And what Lucian presses upon him is just the old Sceptic argument from the disagreement of the schools. How did Hermotimus know in the first instance which guide, out of all those who offered, he should choose to follow ? How could he estimate the value of the different schools without having already the knowledge he was setting out to seek ?   The far-off City, whose citizens are all blissful and righteous, in the radiance of an unearthly peace—ah, if one knew the way thither, would it not be worth while to throw everything else to the winds, to break every tie, in order to reach it !   'Once I heard an old man describing what it is like there, and he exhorted me to follow him to the City.   He would be my guide himself and inscribe my name on its registers, when I came there, and make me a member of one of its tribes and get me admitted to his own phratry, so that I too might be blessed among the blessed.   " *But I hearkened not unto him*," as I was young and foolish then, fifteen years ago. . . . Yes, I myself, Hermotimus, have the same desire in my heart that you have, and there is nothing, if I could have my wish, that I should prefer to this.   If the City were near and plain for everybody to see, be sure that I should have started for it long ago without question and been its citizen now these many years.' [1]   But the way !—that was just

---

[1] Ἤδη γάρ ποτε καὶ ἄλλοτε πρεσβύτου ἀνδρὸς ἤκουσα διεξιόντος ὅπως τὰ ἐκεῖ πράγματα ἔχοι, καί με προὔτρεπεν ἔπεσθαί οἱ πρὸς τὴν πόλιν· ἡγήσεσθαι γὰρ αὐτὸς καὶ ἐλθόντα ἐγγράψειν καὶ φυλέτην ποιήσεσθαι καὶ φρατρίας μεταδώσειν τῆς αὑτοῦ, ὡς μετὰ πάντων εὐδαιμονοίην· 'ἀλλ' ἐγὼ οὐ πιθόμην' ὑπ' ἀνοίας καὶ νεότητος τότε, πρὸ πεντεκαίδεκα σχεδὸν ἐτῶν . . . καὶ γὰρ αὐτός, ὦ Ἑρμότιμε, τῶν αὐτῶν σοι ἐρῶ καὶ οὐκ ἔστιν ὅ τι ἄν μοι πρὸ τούτων εὐξαίμην γενέσθαι. εἰ μὲν

what no one knew, and it was better, the Sceptic convinced Hermotimus, to give up the vain hope and shun the philosopher who stirs it up in one's heart as one would a mad dog.

The doctrines of the old philosophic schools—the soul a fiery vapour, the god that is the ethereal envelope of the Universe, the atoms that fall downwards through infinite space or swerve spontaneously without external cause—any old system as we see it now, looking back, appears so crude, so naïve in many of its assertions, that it would be easy, we feel, for us, if we could enter one of those schools with all our modern knowledge, to show how rashly and absurdly those theories were building upon the void.   But really I don't know that we could say anything more telling or more apt than the old Sceptics did actually say.   The warning voice had sounded out clear to the world and was heard through all the places where men disputed and reasoned ; the four hundred volumes of Hasdrubal-Clitomachus, the compact effective arguments of Aenesidemus, the penetrating irony of Lucian, all these things were there, palpable and audible, during the centuries when the determination of the people of the Greco-Roman world slowly matured to put themselves under the authority of a new dogma.   Men did not answer the Sceptical arguments : they simply went past them, turned their backs upon them.

Why was this ?   Why was the logic of the Sceptics

οὖν πλησίον ἦν ἡ πόλις καὶ φανερὰ ἰδεῖν ἅπασι, πάλαι ἄν, εὖ ἴσθι, μηδὲν ἐνδοιάσας αὐτὸς ᾔειν ἐς αὐτὴν καὶ ἐπολιτευόμην ἂν ἐκ πολλοῦ. Lucian, *Herm.* 24, 25.

impotent to arrest this movement of the human spirit ?
I think that as we look at the history more closely, we
see why. If in the profession of a dogmatic belief the
asserter means 'There is no possibility of my being
mistaken : it is as objectively certain that what I
maintain is true as that any sensation, which you have,
exists as a sensation'; if this is what dogmatism means,
then the Sceptical argument was a complete and un-
answerable refutation of the dogmatic position. And
this is very much what dogmatism did mean, in the
Stoic form. The Wise Man was above any possibility
of error : the *kataleptike phantasia* gave him as certain a
knowledge of the Stoic dogmas as he had that two and
two were four; he would never hold an opinion; he
knew. What the Sceptics proved was that there is
nothing, except sensation—to have been quite thorough
they ought to have said immediately present sensation—
as to the existence of which one must not admit the
abstract possibility of error. Any inference from immediate sensation (we may add, any memory of past
sensation) *may* be a delusion. So far the Sceptics were
logically triumphant. But there was one respect in
which the Sceptical philosophy hopelessly broke down;
it broke down just where all Agnosticism must break
down, before the exigencies of life—before the fact that
man is not only a spectator of Reality, but a maker of
it. If we were minds suspended in space merely
watching what went on, we might well, so far as I can
see, take the advice of the Sceptic to hold back from all
belief; we might simply wait and see what happened.
But we have to act, to-day and to-morrow and all the

days to come. It was, when all was said and done, because men wanted guidance for action that they turned, in spite of all the Sceptics could urge, to dogmatic systems—to Stoicism, to Epicureanism, and later on to Neoplatonism and the Church. There was an imperious need which the dogmatic systems set out to supply, and which Scepticism could neither supply nor set aside. That was felt by the old opponents of Scepticism, when to all the Sceptical arguments they returned ever again the answer that consistent Scepticism would reduce man to inactivity. It was an objection which went home, and which the Sceptics were at great pains to rebut. And their attempt to do so is the most pitiful thing imaginable.

What had Scepticism to say, when men put the question to it, How then were they to live? In reviewing the successive phases of Scepticism, I have put their attempts to answer that question aside in order that we might consider the practical conclusion of the Sceptical philosophy by itself at the end. The answer of Scepticism to that question was in effect : ' Well, you will just do what other people do : you will conform to the usages of society : you will let yourself go with the stream.' Timon, the first exponent of Pyrrhonism in writing, laid stress, as we have seen, on the fact that he had not broken with ordinary conventions (μὴ ἐκβεβηκέναι τὴν συνήθειαν). In the Academy Scepticism was in fusion with another and more aristocratic spirit derived from Plato, and had to find some principle of conduct which seemed less like surrendering one's soul to the common herd, a principle which at any rate represented some individual choice, some autonomy. Arcesilaus, according to our report, found this principle is what approved itself to the agent as reasonable (τὸ εὔλογον), and he seems curiously to have adduced the Stoic definition of a right action as 'that for which, when it has been performed, a reasonable defence can be made'.[1] Probably, this sample of the ethical doctrine of Arcesilaus is merely an *argumentum ad hominem*, a stroke in his standing feud with the Stoics. The Stoics, I think, had been obliged to frame this cumbrous definition of a *kathēkon*, because they wanted to describe it as a reasonable action, whilst on their theory no action could be really reasonable except one performed *phronimōs* by the ideal Wise Man. Arcesilaus seems to have caught it up and said : ' Very well, if you admit that an action can be reasonable in a sense, although not performed with the perfect

---

[1] 'Αλλ' ἐπεὶ μετὰ τοῦτο ἔδει καὶ περὶ τῆς τοῦ βίου διεξαγωγῆς ζητεῖν, ἥτις οὐ χωρὶς κριτηρίου πέφυκεν ἀποδίδοσθαι, ἀφ' οὗ καὶ ἡ εὐδαιμονία, τουτέστι τὸ τοῦ βίου τέλος, ἠρτημένην ἔχει τὴν πίστιν, φησὶν ὁ 'Αρκεσίλαος ὅτι οὐ περὶ πάντων ἐπέχων κανονιεῖ τὰς αἱρέσεις καὶ φυγὰς καὶ κοινῶς τὰς πράξεις τῷ εὐλόγῳ, κατὰ τοῦτό τε προερχόμενος τὸ κριτήριον κατορθώσει· τὴν μὲν γὰρ εὐδαιμονίαν περιγίνεσθαι διὰ τῆς φρονήσεως, τὴν δὲ φρόνησιν κινεῖσθαι ἐν τοῖς κατορθώμασιν, τὸ δὲ κατόρθωμα εἶναι ὅπερ πραχθὲν εὔλογον ἔχει τὴν ἀπολογίαν. ὁ προσέχων οὖν τῷ εὐλόγῳ κατορθώσει καὶ εὐδαιμονήσει. Sext. Emp. *adv. math.* vii. 158.

Cf. Ἔτι δὲ καθῆκόν φασιν (the Stoics) εἶναι ὃ πραχθὲν εὔλογον ἴσχει ἀπολογισμόν· οἷον τὸ ἀκόλουθον ἐν τῇ ζωῇ, ὅπερ καὶ ἐπὶ τὰ φυτὰ καὶ ζῷα διατείνει. Diog. Laert. vii, § 107. Ὁρίζεται δὲ τὸ καθῆκον· τὸ ἀκόλουθον ἐν ζωῇ, ὃ πραχθὲν εὔλογον ἀπολογίαν ἔχει· παρὰ τὸ καθῆκον δὲ τὸ ἐναντίως. τοῦτο διατείνει καὶ εἰς τὰ ἄλογα τῶν ζῴων, ἐνεργεῖ γάρ τι κἀκεῖνα ἀκολούθως τῇ ἑαυτῶν φύσει· ἐπὶ δὲ τῶν λογικῶν ζῴων οὕτως ἀποδίδοται· τὸ ἀκόλουθον ἐν βίῳ. Stob. *Ecl.* ii. 7, 8, p. 85, Wachsmuth.

knowledge possessed by the Wise Man, that is all I want as a guide for action, and you cannot urge against my philosophy that it has made all principle for action impossible.' This does not tell us what Arcesilaus himself understood by 'the reasonable', and in default of further explanation we have only a formal phrase without definite content.

Nor when we come to his brilliant successor Carneades do we get any clearer guidance. Carneades had, as we saw, his theory of graduated probability, which was to be applied to practice, but one cannot gather any definite principles of conduct that Carneades himself suggested as the ones to be followed. Of course, all action implies judgements of two kinds, judgements as to what the existing data are, 'existential' judgements, and judgements as to what ought to be, as to the new reality to be constituted by our action, value-judgements. In both sorts of judgement the Wise Man would, according to Carneades, follow probability; he would form an opinion as to phenomena and their concatenation, and an opinion as to the Good to be realized. But when an instance is given us, it is only a judgement of the first kind; the Wise Man, we are told, would embark on a vessel in virtue of a judgement that it would probably arrive at its destination. When we ask what Carneades took the Good to be, the end to be aimed at in action, we get no answer. Carneades showed a keen debating interest in the positive doctrines of the different schools; he loved to take one or other of them as a thesis, whose strength he could exhibit with all his forensic cleverness, turning round next to defend the opposite view with equal ability. It was he who mapped out the scheme under which all possible answers to the question, 'What is the good?' could be logically classified (the 'Carneadia divisio').[1] But to any view of his own on that cardinal question he does not seem to have committed himself, nor are we, by scrutinizing the fragments of his teaching which have come down to us, likely to succeed in enucleating one, since even Clitomachus, his assiduous reporter, admitted that he had never been able to discover what his master really thought.[2]

The later sceptics, Aenesidemus and his line, fell back upon the principle stated at the outset by Timon, convention (συνήθεια). The Sceptic rule of practice is clearly explained by Sextus Empiricus. 'We attend to the appearance of things (ta phainomena) and live a human life, observing the conditions of such a life, without holding

---

[1] 'Quod quoniam in quo sit (i.e. in what the *summum bonum* consists) magna dissensio est, Carneadia nobis adhibenda divisio est . . . Ille igitur vidit non modo quot fuissent adhuc philosophorum de summo bono, sed quot omnino esse possent, sententiae.' Cic. *De Fin.* v. 16. According to this 'divisio' there are nine possible conceptions of the *summum bonum*—six simple ones, (1) Pleasure, maintained by Aristippus, (2) Absence of pain, maintained by Hieronymus, (3) τὰ πρῶτα κατὰ φύσιν, maintained as a thesis in debate by Carneades himself, (4) the direction of the will towards pleasure, apart from attainment, a view *sine patrono*, (5) the direction of the will towards absence of pain, apart from attainment, likewise *sine patrono*, (6) the direction of the will towards τὰ πρῶτα κατὰ φύσιν, apart from attainment, the view of the Stoics, who identify this, direction of the will with Virtue; and three double ones (1) Pleasure *plus* virtue, maintained by Calliphon and Dinomachus, (2) absence of pain *plus* virtue, maintained by the Peripatetic Diodorus of Tyre, (3) τὰ πρῶτα κατὰ φύσιν *plus* virtue, maintained by the ordinary Peripatetics and older Academy.

[2] Cic. *Ac.* ii. § 139.

any opinion, since we cannot give up action altogether. This observation of the conditions of life seems to come under four heads; firstly, there is the way marked out by Nature, by which we are so constituted as to have certain sensations and thoughts; secondly, there is the compulsion of our bodily feelings, the hunger that drives us to food, the thirst that drives us to drink, and so on; thirdly, there is the tradition embodied in customs and laws, by which we are taught as a matter of practical life (βιωτικῶς) that religion is a good thing and irreligion a bad thing; and, lastly, there is technical instruction, by which we can maintain our activity in the various arts and crafts that have come down to us. But in saying all this we imply no opinion as to truth.'[1] 'We follow life (*bios*, the ordinary ways of society) without opinion, so that we may not give up action.'[2] 'We live following established laws and customs and natural appetites, without opinion.'[3] 'We must think meanly of the

---

[1] Τοῖς φαινομένοις οὖν προσέχοντες κατὰ τὴν βιωτικὴν τήρησιν ἀδοξάστως βιοῦμεν, ἐπεὶ μὴ δυνάμεθα ἀνενέργητοι παντάπασιν εἶναι. ἔοικε δὲ αὕτη ἡ βιωτικὴ τήρησις τετραμερὴς εἶναι καὶ τὸ μέν τι ἔχειν ἐν ὑφηγήσει φύσεως, τὸ δὲ ἐν ἀνάγκῃ παθῶν, τὸ δὲ ἐν παραδόσει νόμων τε καὶ ἐθῶν, τὸ δὲ ἐν διδασκαλίᾳ τεχνῶν, ὑφηγήσει μὲν φυσικῇ καθ' ἣν φυσικῶς αἰσθητικοὶ καὶ νοητικοί ἐσμεν, παθῶν δὲ ἀνάγκῃ καθ' ἣν λιμὸς μὲν ἐπὶ τροφὴν ἡμᾶς ὁδηγεῖ δίψος δ' ἐπὶ πόμα, ἐθῶν δὲ καὶ νόμων παραδόσει καθ' ἣν τὸ μὲν εὐσεβεῖν παραλαμβάνομεν βιωτικῶς ὡς ἀγαθὸν τὸ δὲ ἀσεβεῖν ὡς φαῦλον, τεχνῶν δὲ διδασκαλίᾳ καθ' ἣν οὐκ ἀνενέργητοί ἐσμεν ἐν αἷς παραλαμβάνομεν τέχναις. ταῦτα δὲ πάντα φάμεν ἀδοξάστως. Sext. Emp. *Hyp.* i. 23, 24.

[2] Ἀδοξάστως ἑπομένων τῷ βίῳ, ἵνα μὴ ἀνενέργητοι ὦμεν. ib. 226.

[3] Ἡμεῖς δὲ τοῖς νόμοις καὶ τοῖς ἔθεσι καὶ τοῖς φυσικοῖς πάθεσιν ἑπόμενοι βιοῦμεν ἀδοξάστως. ib. 231.

intelligence of those who suppose that they shut up the
Sceptic to inactivity or self-contradiction,' he says in
another frank passage. 'They fail to see that the
Sceptic does not frame his life as a *man* according to the
doctrine which he professes as a *philosopher*. So far
as he adheres to that, he does not act at all. Only,
noticing in an unphilosophic way how things go, he is
able to choose some things and shun others. Supposing
a tyrant puts constraint upon him to do something
abominable, it may be he will be guided in choosing
and refusing by such notion of what is fitting as is embodied in the laws and customs of the society to which
by birth he belongs. He will also bear hardships more
easily than the man of dogmatic beliefs, because his
sensation will not have an opinion added to it as an
extra (the opinion that his suffering is an evil), as will be
there in the case of the other man.'[1] It seems poor
comfort to a man in pain to tell him that after all he
does not know that his pain is an evil, for the retort is
so obvious that he does not know whether it is not.
But it was the best comfort the Sceptic had to give.
Sextus tries to eke it out by repeating the assertion

---

[1] Ὅθεν καὶ καταφρονεῖν ἀναγκαῖον τῶν εἰς ἀνενεργησίαν αὐτὸν
περικλείεσθαι νομιζόντων ἢ εἰς ἀπέμφασιν . . . ταῦτα δὴ λέγοντες οὐ
συνιᾶσιν ὅτι κατὰ μὲν τὸν φιλόσοφον λόγον οὐ βιοῖ ὁ σκεπτικὸς
(ἀνενέργητος γάρ ἐστιν ὅσον ἐπὶ τούτῳ), κατὰ δὲ τὴν ἀφιλόσοφον
τήρησιν δύναται τὰ μὲν αἱρεῖσθαι τὰ δὲ φεύγειν. ἀναγκαζόμενός τε
ὑπὸ τυράννου τι τῶν ἀπηγορευμένων πράττειν, τῇ κατὰ τοὺς πατρίους
νόμους καὶ τὰ ἔθη προλήψει τυχὸν τὸ μὲν ἑλεῖται τὸ δὲ φεύξεται· καὶ
ῥᾷόν γε οἴσει τὸ σκληρὸν παρὰ τὸν ἀπὸ τῶν δογμάτων, ὅτι οὐδὲν
ἔξωθεν τούτῳ προσδοξάζει καθάπερ ἐκεῖνος. Sext. Emp. *adv. math.* xi.
162-6.

made by Epicurus, that if pain was severe it did not last long, and if it lasted long it was not severe ; but he does not feel quite satisfied with that, since he breaks out in the end: 'Well, and if we do feel very great distress, it is not our fault; we suffer because we must, not because we want to; it is all the fault of Nature, "who careth for no law," as the verse says.'[1] This may be true, but is not very helpful. There is one passage in which Sextus strikes a stronger note, 'What happens to the Sceptic of necessity', he says, ' he accepts bravely.'[2] One cannot quarrel with the 'bravely'; but it implies, of course, a belief in certain values which, if reflected on, carries one far beyond the narrow Sceptical ground.

The regular answer, then, of ancient Scepticism to those who sought from it a guide for conduct was simply to refer them to what happened to be the prevailing practice of their society. So far from furnishing a principle for the criticism and improvement of prevalent convention, it might lend itself to the support of any bad custom. If it liberated the intellect from dogma, it only brought practice the more into bondage. It could not even effectually attack the superstition which dominated so much of the life of the ancient world, since while it was concerned to maintain that every dogma might be false, it had to admit that any superstition might be true. If it would have refused to say

[1] Μέτριος οὖν ἐστι καὶ οὐχ οὕτω φοβερὰ ἡ περὶ τὸν σκεπτικὸν συμβαίνουσα ταραχή. οὐ μὴν ἀλλὰ κἂν μεγίστη τις ᾖ, οὐχ ἡμᾶς αἰτιᾶσθαι δεῖ τοὺς ἀκουσίως καὶ κατ' ἀνάγκην πάσχοντας, ἀλλὰ τὴν φύσιν, "ᾗ νόμων οὐδὲν μέλει". Sext. Emp. adv. math. xi. 156.

[2] Τὸ μὲν κατ' ἀνάγκην συμβαῖνον γεννικῶς δεχόμενος (Sext. Emp. adv. math. 118).

'Credo quia impossibile', it was obliged to say 'Non nego quia ineptum'. If you knew absolutely nothing about God, you had no right to say that the popular mythology was any worse representation of Him than the conceptions of the philosopher. We find, therefore, the whole religious tradition of the ancient state, as a system of ritual and mythological imagery, defended on Sceptical principles. 'The Sceptic', says Sextus, 'will be found acknowledging the gods according to the customs of his country and the laws, and doing everything which tends to their proper worship and reverence, but in the region of philosophic inquiry he makes no rash assertion.'[1]   In Cicero's *De Natura Deorum* the part of the Sceptic is sustained by one who holds the office of *pontifex* in the Roman state. 'I have always defended and will always defend', he explains, 'the traditional ceremonies of religion, and no argument of any one, learned or simple, will ever make me budge from the belief which I have received from our ancestors as to the worship of the immortal gods. . . . If you, as a philosopher, can justify my religion on rational grounds, good : but I am bound to believe our ancestors, even though they give no reason '[2]—and Cotta proceeds by

---

[1] Τάχα γὰρ ἀσφαλέστερος παρὰ τοὺς ὡς ἑτέρως φιλοσοφοῦντας εὑρεθήσεται ὁ σκεπτικός, κατὰ μὲν τὰ πάτρια ἔθη καὶ τοὺς νόμους λέγων εἶναι θεοὺς καὶ πᾶν τὸ εἰς τὴν τούτων θρησκείαν καὶ εὐσέβειαν συντεῖνον ποιῶν, τὸ δ' ὅσον ἐπὶ τῇ φιλοσόφῳ ζητήσει μηδὲν προπετευόμενος. Sext. Emp. *adv. math.* ix. 49.

[2] 'Non enim mediocriter moveor auctoritate tua, Balbe, orationeque ea, quae me in perorando cohortabatur, ut meminissem me et Cottam esse et pontificem ; quod eo, credo, valebat, ut opiniones, quas a maioribus accepimus de dis immortalibus, sacra, caerimonias religionesque defen-

means of the arguments of Carneades and Clitomachus to demolish the proofs which the Stoic has adduced of the Divine government of the world.

The old proud religions of the Greco-Roman world were already, when Sextus wrote, being assailed by an enemy which had caught up the weapons of the philosophic Sceptics, no longer in a mood of academic criticism, but with the passion and intense purpose of a new-found faith. And by Scepticism the old religions tried to paralyse the attack. The defender of Paganism against Christianity in the little dialogue of Minucius is a Sceptic. Just because Nature is dark and the Truth undiscoverable, how much better ' to follow the religious practices handed down to you, to worship the gods whom your parents taught you rather to fear than to know with too close a familiarity, to advance no opinion as to the Divine powers, but to believe the men of old ' ! [1]

---

derem. ego vero eas defendam semper semperque defendi, nec me **ex** ea opinione, quam a maioribus accepi de cultu deorum immortalium, ullius umquam oratio aut docti aut indocti movebit ... habes, Balbe, quid Cotta, quid pontifex sentiat; fac nunc ego intellegam, tu quid sentias, a te enim philosopho rationem accipere debeo religionis, maioribus autem nostris etiam nulla ratione reddita credere.' Cic. *De nat. de.* iii. 5. According to the proper sceptical theory Cotta would not have said ' credere'. The Sceptic of the pure water did not *believe* the ancestral tradition; he only followed it in practice ἀδοξάστως, with no opinion as to its truth or untruth.

[1] 'Cum igitur aut fortuna caeca aut incerta natura sit, quanto venerabilius ac melius antistitem veritatis maiorum excipere disciplinam, religiones traditas colere, deos, quos a parentibus ante imbutus es timere quam nosse familiarius, adorare, nec de numinibus ferre sententiam, sed prioribus credere, qui adhuc rudi saeculo in ipsius mundi natalibus meruerunt deos vel famulos habere vel reges!' Minucius Felix,

But Scepticism brought obviously in the long run more hindrance than help to those who sought its aid. For if it enabled them to safeguard the absurdities of the traditional religion from rational attack, it incapacitated them for attacking anything irrational in the new dogma. It was agnostics of the type of Cicero's Cotta and Caecilius in the dialogue of *Octavius* who prepared the Greco-Roman world to listen without much sense of strangeness to the 'Credo quia impossibile' of Tertullian.

The ancient world then had found no stable equilibrium. It was driven on the one hand by its bitter need towards dogmatic systems, such as the Stoic, and on the other driven back from dogmatism into a scepticism which left it void of counsel. Between the two it swung unhappily for generations. Carneades in his theory of graduated probability might seem to have indicated a central position in which it might have settled. But a life directed by the computation of logical probabilities somehow lacks appeal for the human spirit. If besides these three, dogmatism, scepticism, and the calculation of logical probabilities, there is no other possible attitude of the human mind in the face of this Universe, then there would appear no hope but that the tragedy of the ancient world should be ceaselessly repeated till the story of mankind is done. But is there not another possible attitude, which perhaps was implicit in Christianity from the beginning, though in the formulation of

Octavius 6. Here again we have a conflation of the Sceptic doctrine with the theory of Posidonius as to the divine childhood of the race (see page 117). Caecilius stands for the ordinary educated man of the last days of Paganism, to whose body of ideas the old Scepticism and old dogmatism have alike contributed.

Christianity the dogmatic, too exclusively intellectual, habit of the Greek world obscured and mistook it? What account, for instance, is to be given of the belief, the loyal confidence, which a man has in his friend? It has surely a certainty as intensely real as the certainty of the dogmatist, and yet if the man represented tha certainty as one of inerrant logical deduction, a mathe matical certainty, it would be easy for the Sceptic t show the logical possibilities of error at every turn The very gaps of logical proof which the Sceptic might point out give room for the moral assurance to hold its own, rejoicing: if in friendship we walked all through by sight, and never by faith, what scope would there be for trust? For that trust a friend could tolerate no weaker word than certainty. He would repel even the suggestion that in his attitude to the man he loved he should be guided by a careful computation of prob- abilities. Certainty? Yes: but if he represented that certainty to be the same as logical, as mathematical certainty, he would put himself in the wrong and be given defenceless into the hand of the Sceptic. And that mistake, I suggest, is just such a mistake as the ancient dogmatists made in defining their attitude to the great Friend behind the Universe, just such a mistake as was made by their successors whose task it was to formulate the faith of the Christian Church.